Working in London & the UK

plus Ireland, the Netherlands and Malta

for Australians and New Zealanders

Bryan Havenhand
and contributors

Global Exchange
Newcastle

Working in London and the UK plus Ireland, the Netherlands and Malta

First published 1999

Published by
Global Exchange Pty Ltd (A.C.N. 006 887 556)
PO Box 852
Newcastle NSW 2300
Australia
Tel: (02) 4929 4688
Fax: (02) 4929 4727
Email: info@globalexchange.com.au
Web: www.globalexchange.com.au (available soon)

Cover design by Rob Thom Design, Melbourne.
Front cover photograph provided by the British Tourist Authority.
Text design and layout by Anna Kaemmerling, Global Exchange, Newcastle.
Printed in Australia by the Australian Print Group, Maryborough.

National Library of Australia
Cataloguing-in-Publication data:
Havenhand, Bryan
Working in London and the UK plus Ireland, the Netherlands and Malta
for Australians and New Zealanders

Bibliography.
Includes index.
ISBN 1 876438 04 5

1. Australians - Employment - Great Britain. 2. New Zealanders - Employment - Great Britain. I . Title

331. 1250941

Acknowledgements

Like most books this one has numerous silent contributors including all those on the receiving end of letters, faxes, emails and telephone calls. Many thanks to those who replied with information, ideas and encouragement. Thanks to *TNT Magazine* in London for the use of some of their material and YHA UK for the article 'A Taste of London'. A special thanks to Wendy Alexander who made this book more readable than it otherwise would have been. Thanks also to my wife Anna who did the text layout and put up with my long days.

Editor

Bryan Havenhand gave up teaching marketing and tourism subjects at TAFE and university to concentrate on developing good resource material for Australians and New Zealanders wanting to work or learn overseas. This first edition of *Working in London & the UK plus Ireland, the Netherlands and Malta* is another step in that direction.

Contributors

Philip Trott and **Peter Moss** specialise in UK Immigration and nationality matters.

Belinda Cranston has a BA from the University of Adelaide and currently resides in Melbourne where she works as a freelance writer in addition to being a part-time previewer on Channel 31. While working in London Belinda worked as a 'headhunter' for two financial services recruitment firms. She later travelled in Switzerland, Egypt and Israel where she worked on a kibbutz.

Peter Barr is a freelance journalist from Perth who sells alcohol when not working or travelling. He has travelled the world (well, a part of it) for five years and has tried to learn something about it, and himself. He's not sure if he has succeeded because he's still constantly confused by both. Peter enjoys reading, writing, golfing, surfing and, at least most of the time, life.

Heather Farish has had numerous articles published in magazines and newspapers throughout Australia. In between exploring foreign lands she spends time trying to motivate young people to travel while teaching them maths and science in country Victoria.

Murry Hedgcock is a sports journalist based in London. He contributes to *The Australian* on a regular basis.

Jeannie Zakharov worked as a journalist in London for four years and currently works in Sydney on a major national newspaper.

Susan Griffith is a well known author with Vacation Work Publications in the United Kingdom. She is author of *Work Your Way Around the World, Teaching English Abroad,* co-author of other titles including *The Au Pair and Nanny Guide to Working Abroad* and author of many articles on working overseas.

Diane Hoggins is an addicted traveller who's articles on travel have featured in a wide range of publications. She is now based in Sydney where she teaches English to overseas students as well as being involved with intercultural programs. She also runs adult education courses on various aspects of travel including working overseas and travel writing and photography.

Margaret Toohey spent two years wandering the globe, and now juggles freelance writing with retailing maps and travel guides in Melbourne while planning her next trip.

Kerry Martin is a journalist and communications consultant. She has lived and worked in several Asian countries and the Netherlands. Kerry is currently landlocked in Melbourne with her new born son, Alexander.

Global Exchange

Global Exchange is a publisher specialising in international work opportunities for Australians and New Zealanders. Other titles in this series are:

Working Overseas: a working holiday guide for Australians and New Zealanders (3rd ed)

Teaching Overseas for Australians and New Zealanders (2nd ed)

Volunteer Work Overseas for Australians and New Zealanders

Japan: a working holiday guide for Australians and New Zealanders

Overseas Recruitment Directory (annual)

Feedback

Global Exchange is always looking for stories and information from travellers who travel a little outside the mainstream. This and other guides will be updated in the future and any material or stories from readers or others will be gratefully received. If your material is used in the next edition of this or another title, you will be mentioned and receive a free copy of the publication. Lengthy contributions also receive payment. The address and contact numbers for Global Exchange are listed above.

Have a great time travelling!

Using this book

The dollar figures in this book are in Australian dollars unless otherwise indicated.

The international telephone and fax numbers shown in this book do not include the country code. The country code for the UK is 44. If ringing or faxing an overseas number, drop the 0 from the regional code shown in this book (i.e. 0171 becomes 171). The international code for Australia is 0011 (telephone) and 0015 (fax) and for New Zealand, 00 or 1600 if you wish to make a Price Required Call.

Email and website addresses in this book finish with a full stop. This is only a convention and should not be used when using an email or web address.

If you intend downloading information from websites please note that you need to be sure that the site is secure and doesn't allow viruses onto your machine. Global Exchange takes no responsibility for this possibility.

Contents

Ireland, the Netherlands, Malta

More information

Time to go

Bryan Havenhand

Go for it—sell yourself, you can do anything and be anything over there. It just takes some 'get up and go' and courage—the confidence comes later. (Kathy Roberts, a returned working-holiday maker.)

You're getting itchy feet, your job is boring you, friends of yours have already taken the plunge and have sent back glowing reports, your relationship has broken up, adventure beckons, your contract has ended ... There are endless reasons to begin thinking about working overseas. Well, end the dreaming, it's easier than you think. It's time to go.

There is no easier place to work overseas than the UK (especially if you are between the ages of 17 and 27). The locals speak English (and they can usually understand the twang and slang of antipodeans), Australian and New Zealand qualifications are mostly recognised (sometimes with additional paperwork), antipodeans, along with South Africans, have a good reputation as workers (this will surprise some) and there is an infrastructure (employment agencies, media, social clubs, accommodation options) to support those from down-under. In fact, so extensive are these networks, that if you are not careful you will miss meeting the locals altogether, which is surely one of the reasons for going.

The working holiday visa for the UK has been available to Australians and New Zealanders since time immemorial and other types of visas are available for those with claims to British ancestry. Likewise, there are many UK citizens working in Australia and New Zealand. Although the working holiday visa is available to those over 17, it is recommended that you don't go until you are somewhat older. Jobs are easier to obtain if you have some qualifications and experience. The UK, and London in particular, is an expensive place to live, so those working for minimum wages will not have much to spend on anything beyond the basic necessities of rent, food and transport. With so much happening around you, especially in London, you'll certainly want some spare readies to indulge yourself.

The UK Department of Immigration estimates that some 80,000 Australians and 40,000 New Zealanders are currently working in the UK, mostly in London. Each year about 15,000 Australians and 8000 New Zealanders go on the working holiday visa along with those on other types of visas that permit work (mostly ancestral visas). Of course, not having a work visa has not stopped anyone. About 660,000 Australians and 140,000 New Zealanders travel on tourist visas to the UK each year to check out castles, the culture, the entertainment and to catch up with friends and family, among other things.

There will be lots happening in London either side of the millennium (both the lead up to the year 2000 and the lead up to the real millennium year, 2001). New art galleries, like the new Tate Gallery of Modern Art, the new Wellcome Wing at the Science Museum and the Millennium Dome will all be opening with great fanfare. London will excel itself in welcoming the new century, which means interesting times for residents and visitors.

This book also provides information on working in Ireland, the Netherlands and Malta, all of which provide working holiday visas to Australians. Ireland also has a working holiday visa for New Zealand. The work opportunities in these countries are small in number compared to those in the UK, but some people may be attracted to these destinations for other reasons.

So, whether you choose the UK or one of these other destinations for your working holiday, make the most of your opportunities, and go for it!

Getting ready to go

Bryan Havenhand

When to go

If you have control over when you go to the UK then there are some points worth considering.

Maybe you want to avoid arriving in winter. The weather in London is such that Melbournians never complain about Melbourne weather again. (I've lived in Melbourne for quite a few years so that is not a cheap shot.) No doubt the same could be said for those living in Wellington. The UK summer sun is usually a bit insipid and doesn't provide much heat, though there are exceptions like the summer of 1994 which was a scorcher. Winter dampness wets the bones and never-ending grey skies can extract your enthusiasm for life. No doubt it has driven more than one antipodean home early. It is easy to forget that London is really a long way north. There are only two cities with a population greater than five million that lie north of the 50° parallel—London is one and the other is Moscow. However, London and the UK are saved from having a 'Russian' climate by the Gulf Stream which brings warm water and moderating conditions year round.

The tourist season in London runs from mid-April to mid-October but it is in June, July and August when antipodeans are shivering down-under that the tourists arrive in serious numbers. The population of Greater London (this includes the City of London, the City of Westminster, and inner and outer London) is about seven million, or about nine million if you include the Home Counties that surround Greater London. To provide an idea of how crowded it gets, about 17 million tourists visit the UK each year and a great many spend a good part of their time in the City of London and the City of Westminster. In addition about 350,000 locals work in the City of London (although only about 5,000 live there). Like all tourist destinations at peak time, things get more expensive but lots of extra hands are required to cope with the numbers.

Around the world people like to take their annual holidays during summer and the Brits are no different. The gaps they leave behind are filled by temporary workers who don't mind working during the summer. Unlike Australia, which tends to doze during the peak summer holiday month, London keeps going.

Tertiary students in the UK break from mid-December to mid-January for the Christmas holidays and take up temporary positions in large retail stores leading up to the Christmas rush and January sales. If you are closer to 17 than 27 and wish to work in a retail environment you'd need to arrive early to secure a position at this busy time of the year. There is also lots of extra work in warehousing and distribution leading up to Christmas. Demand for hospitality staff can build towards Christmas as businesses and other organisations begin the pre-Christmas and end-of-year party period.

If you are planning to teach then the school terms may determine when you go. There are three terms beginning with the autumn term from early September to Christmas, spring term from early January to about mid-April, and summer term from early May to the end of July. Likewise, those with an accounting background may benefit from arriving close to the end of the financial year, which in the UK is early April.

Airline prices may be another consideration. These vary between low season, low shoulder, high shoulder and peak: you can guess that peak is when everyone wants to travel. These times vary with the destination, so peak season to Europe is mid to late December while low is mid-January to the end of February. These seasons are separated by specific dates so plan ahead to pay less. Your travel agent can provide details. Regardless of your outbound price you can usually return in any season.

Passports

Australians can pick up a passport application form from any post office or from the Passport Office of the Department of Foreign

Affairs and Trade in their relevant state capital city. You will need to return the application in person; if you go through the post office, check to see if you need an appointment. The post office takes longer than the Passport Office (up to six weeks). You will need an original full birth certificate from the Registry of Births, Deaths and Marriages in your state or territory. This can take some time, so apply early. You will also need two identical passport-size photographs (that are not too dark and not too light). A passport for an adult is valid for 10 years, and a child's is valid for five years. An adult passport will cost $126. The toll free number for information about Australian passports is 131 232.

New Zealand passports are issued by the Department of Internal Affairs and your travel agent should have an application form. You will need two identical photographs and an original full birth certificate which is available from the Registrar of Births, Deaths and Marriages for NZ$15. Processing of passports takes from 10 working days to six weeks. Passports are valid for 10 years and cost NZ$80.

If you have a parent or grandparent born in the UK or Ireland then you may be eligible for a British or Irish passport, which will have the advantage of opening up your work opportunities. If you are able to gain one of these passports it will also allow you to work in other EU countries with some conditions. See chapter 5 and chapter 20 for more details.

If you already have a passport make sure it's valid for the time you plan to spend away plus six months. Some countries will not allow entry if less than six months validity remains on the passport. You can arrange to renew your passport if it expires while you are overseas by going to your nearest consular office. If you no longer look like your passport photo, think about having a new one taken, particularly if you intend to be away for some time. If you are an Australian with dual citizenship you must leave and enter Australia on your Australian passport.

Australian citizens will find it worth checking the website of the Australian Foreign Affairs and Trade Department at www.dfat.gov.au/ for up-to-date information on passports and a range of other issues. You might also want to read the Consular Newsletter at www.dfat.gov.au/consular/newsletter. This newsletter includes reports received from Australian travellers at overseas consulates.

Likewise for New Zealanders, the website of the Ministry of Foreign Affairs and Trade is at www.mfat.govt.nz/; follow 'travelling overseas' to find the relevant information. Consular notices can be found at www.mfat.govt.nz/travel/consular.html. For passport information go to http://identity-services.dia.govt.nz/identity.html. This page is part of the website of the Department of Internal Affairs.

Visas

This section covers the key elements of work visa requirements for the UK; more detailed information can be found in chapter 5. Australians are also eligible for working holiday visas to Ireland, the Netherlands and Malta and these visas are covered in chapter 20. New Zealanders are eligible for working holiday visas to Ireland.

There are four main types of visas that will allow you to work in the UK: working holiday visas, visas based on ancestry, work visas sponsored by an employer and visas obtainable under various programs, often authorised by The Work Experience Scheme (TWES). TWES is covered in chapter 4. Sponsored work visas require an employer who will sponsor the applicant on the basis of their special skills or qualifications which are not available locally. This sponsorship is most often job specific and requires the employer, not the potential employee, to lodge the application with the UK immigration authorities. It is now possible for Australian and New Zealand teachers to obtain employer sponsorship on the basis of the increasing difficulty that the UK education system has in finding sufficient teachers. This problem has already arisen in New Zealand and will, no doubt, soon arise in Australia. One organisation offering this service is Teach UK.

There are two types of visas based on ancestry, more properly called a 'Certificate of Entitlement to the Right of Abode' and 'United

Kingdom Ancestry Entry Clearance'. Without going into detail, the first allows you to convert to a British passport and places no work restrictions on the holder, while the second places no work restrictions on the holder but it is valid for four years only. There is usually a great deal of paper work required to obtain these visas. If you have a parent or grandparent born in the UK then you might be eligible for one of these visas, in which case you should contact the visa section of the British High Commission for further information.

The most popular visa is the working holiday visa. The key eligibility requirements are that you:

- have Australian or New Zealand citizenship (i.e. eligible for a passport)
- be aged between 17 and 27 years
- visit primarily for a holiday, not employment (you are not allowed to work for more than half your stay in the UK)
- be single or a married couple where both partners are eligible for the visa
- be able to support and accommodate yourself without British welfare
- leave at the end of the two year period allowed by the visa
- provide evidence of having at least, in the case of Australians, $3000 and in the case of New Zealanders, a one-way ticket and the equivalent of £2000 or a return ticket and £1500.

Those with children who meet the criteria must leave the UK before the child turns five years old. Working holiday-makers are not allowed to take full-time work, defined as more than 25 hours per week, for more than half their stay. This can mean either full-time work for shorter periods or part-time work for longer periods. The definition of full-time work as being 25 hours per week (if only we were so lucky) is intended to prevent those on a working holiday visa applying for a real full-time job (i.e. 35-40 hours per week). While it is still possible to make a direct application to an employer for a short-term position, in reality most antipodeans make use of recruitment agencies to find work.

You are not able to take employment that represents a continuation of your career with specific exceptions being made for agency nursing, nannies, occupational therapists, physiotherapists, vets, radiographers, speech therapists and supply (casual) teachers. In reality there is also a huge demand in London for those who work in IT and the finance area, especially accountants, and there is no shortage of short-term work for them. The type of position you take in the UK relative to your qualifications and experience is something you may need to discuss with the agency you chose to work with. There are arguably many grey areas. For example, is an architect who fills a temporary drafting position or a qualified accountant working as a temporary bookkeeper continuing their career?

The working holiday visa begins to tick over from the date of first entry to the UK, so it is no longer possible to visit other countries and put your visa on 'hold' while you're out of the UK. You should enter the UK within six months of the issuing of the visa otherwise without special arrangements it lapses. In Australia the charge for the working holiday visa is $104.70 including postage and in New Zealand it is NZ$107.25.

In Australia contact: Visa Section, British High Commission, 10th Floor, CBS Tower, Cnr Akuna and Bunda Streets, Canberra 2601. Tel. (02) 6257 1982 or 1902 941 555 (24-hour information and ordering line). Fax: (02) 6257 5857. Website: www.uk.emb.gov.au. In New Zealand contact: Visa Section, British High Commission, 44 Hill Street, Wellington. Tel: (04) 495 0848. Fax: (04) 471 1974. There is an information line on (04) 472 6049. Website: www.brithighcomm.org.nz.

If you intend to travel to other countries check with your travel agent regarding the visa requirements for each country. To be on the safe side make sure these visas allow multiple-entry and are not single entry visas. Multiple entry visas allow you in and out of a country more than once. Also, be aware of time limits as some visas require you to arrive before a certain date, and some start to run when you receive the visa instead of when you first arrive in the country. Remember a visa is not a guarantee that you can enter a country. The final say rests with the immigration officials who meet you on arrival. So it is worthwhile dressing conservatively and behaving in a cooperative manner.

Dual citizenship

If you, your parents or, in some cases, your grandparents were born in another country, you may be entitled to residency status in that country, or even to a passport. Clearly those antipodeans who have access to another passport are at a great advantage when it comes to finding work overseas. Especially those who possess a passport to a country which is a member of the European Union as it allows the holder to work in any of the 15 member states. Australia and New Zealand recognise dual citizenship but not all countries do. If you are in a position to obtain the passport of another country, make sure it doesn't compromise your existing passport. This issue should not be a problem if you are eligible for a British or Irish passport.

Airline tickets

The type of ticket you purchase will depend on your plans. One-way fares are expensive, well over half the cost of a return fare; return tickets will have an expiry date which is usually 12 months. If you intend to stay longer without returning home you should discuss ticket options with your travel agent. The cheaper the ticket the more inflexible it becomes in terms of altering bookings at a later date and the longer it may take to get to your destination. Higher priced tickets fly a more direct route and are more likely to have greater flexibility. It may be worth paying more for a ticket with fewer restrictions if you are uncertain of your plans.

With frequent flyer schemes within the reach of most passengers these days, you might want to sign up for one of these schemes before you take off. At the least you'll get a free domestic flight upon return home for a small annual fee. World airlines are beginning to coalesce into alliances, two of which are up and running, Star Alliance and Oneworld. In order to maximise your frequent flyer points you should, where possible, choose an alliance and fly only those airlines. Oneworld consists of Qantas, British Airways, Cathay Pacific, American Airlines and Canadian Airlines. Star Alliance consists of Ansett, Air New Zealand, Singapore Airlines, Lufthansa, United Airlines, Air Canada, Varig, Thai Airways and SAS. Put the cost of the ticket onto your credit card and gain additional points.

Travel insurance and medical cover

The saying 'If you can't afford travel insurance then you can't afford to travel' amounts to good advice. Travellers should always make sure they have adequate travel insurance which covers a range of possibilities from medical problems to loss of luggage. The problem for those who intend to spend time working is that most travel insurance policies will not cover you when working. While legitimate employment will include some sort of workers' compensation, clearly illegal employment will not. So if you are working odd jobs, getting compensation as a result of an accident can be a difficult and slow process. Because of a lack of insurance cover at work and because of reciprocal health care arrangements with the UK, some recommend that you don't take out travel insurance. However, if you intend to travel between periods of work it is best to err on the safe side and purchase a travel insurance policy. This can be done before leaving home (which should cover you for cancellation, return home due a death or serious illness in the family, or repatriation) or it can be taken out in the UK which means it will repatriate you to the UK, not home.

Both Australia and New Zealand have reciprocal health care arrangements with the UK. Australians need to have their valid Medicare card and passport to access these benefits. New Zealanders should have their passport. Advise medical staff at the time of treatment that you wish to be treated under the Reciprocal Health Care Agreement with Australia or New Zealand.

You will be treated as an NHS (National Health Service) patient, but note that doctors are not obliged to accept NHS patients. If you pay a private consultation fee this will not be refundable unless you have a National Insurance number. You'll therefore need to find a doctor willing to treat you or, otherwise, visit an outpatient department of a public hospital. You'll also have access to a public ward in an NHS hospital for emergency treatment. To obtain the latest information Australians should pick up the 'Thinking of travelling overseas?' brochure from a Medicare office or ring 132 011. New Zealanders should contact the Visa Section of the British High Commission.

Questions to ask when choosing travel insurance:

- If you had to cancel your trip, what cover would be available for loss of deposit or ticket payment and other cancellation charges?
- What type of medical and hospital cover is included and what is the maximum cover?
- Does it cover existing medical conditions?
- Do you intend to undertake sports like scuba diving or skiing?
- What if you were injured and needed to fly home?
- Does it cover the airfare home if there is a death or serious illness in the family?
- Is there a 24-hour contact phone number for emergencies?
- What public liability is included? If you intend spending time in the US, this type of cover is vital given the fondness for litigation in this country.
- How much are your goods worth and do you want to cover them all? Be careful of 'averaging' provisions.
- What is the maximum payout per item?
- Will the policy cover things you buy overseas?
- Will the policy cover cash?

- Will it cover items stolen from a car, including the boot?
- What excesses are payable for claims?
- Can you make claims at overseas offices?
- Can the policy be extended while you are overseas and can this be done on your behalf?
- Will the policy cover you while you are working as a paid or volunteer worker?

Remember the more comprehensive and generous the policy, the more expensive it will be. Choose one that is appropriate for your needs.

Pre-booked accommodation

This is strongly recommended; refer to chapter 9.

Medical matters

It's a good idea to have any dental work done before leaving as dental work in the UK is expensive. If you have any doubts about your health have these checked out before you go. If you are on medication take a note from your doctor outlining your condition and have him or her use the generic names of your medication as the brand names of drugs can vary between countries. If you have contact lenses or glasses take the prescription details with you.

If planning to travel outside Western Europe, which is pretty safe from a health point of view, it is wise to check out the health advice and vaccination requirements for the other regions you'll be visiting. Australians can visit one of the Travellers' Medical and Vaccination Centres which provide an extremely comprehensive service and up-to-date information. There is at least one centre in each of the capital cities and another on the Gold Coast. For the cost of a local call Australians can call MASTA on 1300 655 565 to be given the address of a medical practice near to you that has up-to-date information on travel health. There are also other medical practices that have a good knowledge of travel medicine. It is recommended that New Zealanders visit their nearest government Health Development Unit. If you can not get to a large centre, read up on current requirements (Lonely Planet guides are useful for this) before talking to your doctor.

It must be remembered that despite the headlines about lingering malaria and contaminated blood transfusions in outback Africa, most people who die while travelling die from the same conditions that their demographic group dies from at home. Heart attacks kill older people and younger people tend to die from car crashes and other accidents.

Organising your money

You should have as much money as you can muster. Living in London in particular is expensive and unless you have a job lined up before you arrive, it may take a while before you get one. A recent list produced by the Economist Intelligence Unit showed that in 1997 London was ranked 10th among the world's most expensive cities, even though it was only ranked 28th in the previous year. So don't rely on your friend's or aunt's experience five years ago. If you are arriving on a working holiday visa you'll need to meet the minimum financial requirements of the visa, however, having a bit more will give you some breathing space before you get paranoid about spending it all.

Make sure you have a credit card with a decent limit, travellers cheques and a small amount of cash for use at the airport and on the first day. You can cash Thomas Cook travellers cheques in the UK for no charge at either stand-alone Thomas Cook outlets or in Midland Banks where Thomas Cook operates the bureau de change. American Express travellers cheques can be cashed without commission at either American Express offices or at Lloyds Bank. The alternative to taking travellers cheques is to open a bank account in London through your bank at home before you leave. See what your bank can organise. More on this in chapter 11.

Like at home, MasterCard, Visa, Diners Club and American Express are all widely accepted in the UK but, unlike home, businesses can charge an additional amount for taking a payment on credit card. If you maintain your credit card account at home you'll need to organise for it to be paid each month. Remember that when foreign currency moves through your credit card there is a charge and this can add up. Taking MasterCard as an example: any purchases made in US dollars will be converted into Australian dollars and debited to your account. However, any purchases not made in US dollars (e.g. £) will first be converted to US dollars and then to Australian dollars. If choosing a credit card to use overseas you may wish to clarify this aspect of card use and find out what costs are involved.

Look after your card and be on the lookout for credit card scams. Make sure you obtain the latest number to ring in the UK if you lose your card. You can also sign up to Credit Card Sentinel before leaving home. You are able to leave details of all your cards (credit and others) with Credit Card Sentinel and one phone call can have them report the loss of all your cards and organise the replacement of some of them. In Australia telephone 1800 022 043 for more details.

Visa TravelMoney is a useful pre-paid, PIN-protected card which allows you to withdraw cash in the local currency, 24 hours a day. You can use your card at ATMs around the world. The minimum card value is $250 and the maximum is $10,000; once you have spent the money the card is useless. If there is money remaining on the card it can be withdrawn upon return home. You are able to take additional cards, which is helpful in the case of theft. Visa TravelMoney can be purchased from Thomas Cook, Citibank or selected Australia Post offices.

If you find yourself in need of emergency cash, you can arrange for someone to send money through Travelex. Travelex will convert cash into the required currency and transfer it to the nearest Western Union branch of the country you are in. This can be done in 40 minutes. In Australia telephone 1800 649 565 for more information.

Keeping in touch with home

No longer restricted to letters and the odd phone call, keeping in touch with home is easier than it has ever been courtesy of the multiplicity of telephone services and email. Despite the instantaneous link ups available through the telephone and chatrooms on the Internet, everyone enjoys a letter. If you are without a permanent or reliable address have letters sent to you c/- Post Restante, Trafalgar Square Post Office, 24-28 William IV St, London WC2N. Mail will be held for four weeks and you'll require a passport or some other identification when picking up mail. The nearest underground is Charing Cross. American Express and Thomas Cook will generally hold mail, but if you do not have their travellers cheques or card, they will usually charge you for this convenience.

International phone calls home are not cheap but the international phone call business is competitive and there are many deals worth looking at, both at home and overseas. There are some cards and arrangements you can make before leaving home.

The first is to consider the purchase of a mobile phone, which must be a digital (not analogue) phone that uses the international GSM (Global System for Mobile). A mobile phone must have a personal identification number (PIN) in case of theft. Talk to telephone companies about what they have to offer including the British company, Vodafone. Their Australian mobile digital service can be contacted on 008 651 008. (There will be an equivalent number in New Zealand.) Find out the cost of international calls using your own phone so you can compare these with other options. Remember that using a mobile will usually mean you are charged the rates of the country you are calling from, which can be expensive. When calling Australia these rates will vary from around $2 per minute in the UK to around $6 per minute in France, so make sure you know the local charges and also check the time variations. (Telephone companies in the UK are offering prices as low as 12p per minute to Australia and not much more to New Zealand.) Vodafone has one of the most extensive international networks in the world. The main countries not in the network are the US and Japan.

If you intend to use the public phones, Telstra provide Australians with a number of options: Telecard, Phoneaway, International Homelink and the 0018 number for use when those from home want to call you. The Telecard debits the cost of your calls to your home account in Australian dollars and can be accessed in 65 countries around the world. It has a PIN which you select and can change at any time. Freecall 1800 038 000 for more information. Phoneaway is a pre-paid card which can be recharged using a credit card and accessed in over 40 overseas countries. Calls to Australia are billed at Australian rates. These cards are available from Telstra shops, post offices and most newsagents. International Homelink can be accessed in more than 30 other countries. You can call from most phones (privately owned pay phones may require a coin) and, using a special access number and PIN, you'll be automatically connected to your home phone with the call being billed to that account. There is a verification charge plus the normal international direct charge (not the more expensive reverse charge rates). Family and friends at home can call you overseas using Telstra's 0018 (instead of 0011) number in order to keep phone call costs under control. This option provides 'pips' at the 20 minute mark to allow the caller to hang up at 30 minutes. For more information telephone 1800 052 052.

Australians will find that Optus has similar options to those available from Telstra. For more information call Optus on 1300 300 937. If friends and family wish to call you from Australia on a regular basis, there are plenty of very competitive operators offering cut-rate deals to the UK (and just about everywhere else). The prices are continually changing, so if you wish check out all the operators just before you go, including Telstra, Optus, AAPT, One.Tel, Primus GlobeTalk, RSL Com, and WorldxChange.

Telecom New Zealand provides the NZ Direct service for New Zealanders which has two options. You can dial New Zealand yourself and charge it to your Telecom Calling Card or you can talk to a Telecom New Zealand operator who'll place a Calling Card call, collect or credit card, for you. The call is charged at the current international standard or economy rate at the time of calling plus a surcharge as follows: NZ$2.80 for a direct dial Calling Card call; NZ$3.50 for an operator assisted Calling Card or credit card call; and NZ$6.75 for collect calls. For full details call Telecom New Zealand toll free on 0800 803 300.

Once you are in the UK there are many telephone companies competing for your business. See chapter 11 for more information.

Another option is to rent a voicemail box, which is particularly useful if you are travelling. This arrangement allows you to leave messages for those who call, who in turn can leave messages for you. You are able to call and update your outgoing message and check the messages left for you. You pay a fee for the 'mail box' as well as normal telephone charges.

Using email is an increasingly popular and easy-to-use option. If you don't have your own computer and connection to the telephone system make use of one of the many cybercafes that abound. Many public libraries also have an Internet room. You should set up your own email account before leaving home, though you can do this easily in London (or elsewhere). Don't assume you'll be able to access a private email address from a cybercafe, as this is usually not the case. The largest free public email provider is hotmail but if you would like to use something other than Microsoft there are many options including www.yahoo.com, http://email.iycos.com and www.rocketmail.com. The electronic journal www.journeywoman.com provides a free email service for women at www.HERmail.com. The journal is a good site for exchange of information between women travellers. Only recently established is eKno. In association with Lonely Planet, eKno is able to offer free web-based email along with voicemail and telephone calls, all in the one package. For more details see the websites www.ekno.lonelyplanet.com or www.lonelyplanet.com.

For a full list of cybercafes check http://www.cyberiacafe.net/cyberia/guide/cafe.htm or consult the newsgroup at alt.cybercafes. If this all sounds too much, get hold of the *Rough Guide to the Internet & World Wide Web* for a quick familiarisation with how it all works.

Each week *TNT Magazine* publishes a current list of cybercafes in the magazine and also on the TNT website www.tntmag.co.uk. Compare the prices at the different cybercafes as there can be some significant differences, especially in minimum charges, but work on expecting to pay around £6 per hour or £1.50 per 10 minutes.

YHA membership

Membership of the Youth Hostels Association (YHA) allows you to use over 5500 hostels in over 60 countries, which includes 240 hostels in England and Wales and 80 hostels in Scotland. There is no age limit on membership. Even if you don't think you will use it, it is inexpensive and may save you a lot of money if the need arises. It also gives you access to a range of concessions in many countries, in addition to those at home. It is not unusual for those going overseas to rush to a local YHA office to join up a couple of days before leaving. This is a bit silly as a YHA card will give you a range of discounts on goods that you may wish to purchase before you head off. The discount on a good backpack and some walking gear will pay for your membership, which is \$44 plus a \$17 joining fee in Australia and NZ\$34 in New Zealand. More details are available at the YHA's websites www.yha.com.au or www.yha.org.nz.

Discount cards and passes

Discount cards and passes allow you to play tourist in the UK, after all, you'll want to have a break from work sometimes! So to save money, load up with as many cards and passes before you leave home as possible. If you are eligible, the best general purpose discount card for full-time students is the International Student Identity Card (ISIC), which is available from STA Travel offices in Australia and New Zealand. It provides discounts at thousands of locations around the world, including a great many in the UK. Cardholders also have access to a free 24-hour help line. More information can be obtained from the ISTIC website at www.istic.org.

The British Tourist Authority (BTA) is a source of some useful discount cards that should be purchased before leaving home including the London Visitor Travelcard, the Great British Heritage Pass and the London White Card. For $5 in Australia and NZ$7 in New Zealand you can get a package from the BTA which includes loads of information. The cost basically pays for the postage. In Australia send for the 'Britain is full of it' kit and in New Zealand ask for the 'The Big OE Pack'. The addresses are: British Tourist Authority, Level 16, Gateway, 1 Macquarie Place, Sydney 2000 and British Tourist Authority, 17th Floor, Fay Richwhite Bldg, 151 Queen Street, Auckland.

Make sure you get the London Visitor Travelcard, it'll allow you to start to get a fix on the transport system and can be used on both buses and the Underground. There are two cards: the Central Zone card which covers central London, and the All Zone card which covers all of London including Heathrow. Each card is available for either three, four or seven days. Take the seven day card which is currently $53 (Central Zone) or $102 (All Zone).

The London White Card provides unlimited access to 16 museums and galleries. Depending on the exchange rate there may not be much difference between the price of the card at home versus the price in the UK. Check this out before making the purchase.

The Great British Heritage Pass provides entry into about 600 castles, stately homes, gardens and historic sites, most of which are outside London. It is available for seven days, 15 days or one month, and the cost starts at $65 per adult (if you think this sounds expensive wait till you purchase individual tickets in the UK!). Get a copy of the 'Britain: Buy before you go' brochure for a full list of passes, guides, maps and tickets available from the BTA. More details are available at www.visitbritain.bta.org.au.

Another way to access many historic houses and monuments in the UK is to be a member of the National Trust in Australia or New Zealand. This membership allows free or discount entry into National Trust properties in England, Wales and Northern Ireland, and English Heritage and the National Trust of Scotland properties. It does not give you access to Historic Scotland's properties of which there are over 60. This requires the purchase of a separate pass once you are in Scotland.

There are also passes for trains and buses which can result in significant savings if purchased before leaving. Ask your travel agent for information on these. These include the Britrail pass for both youth and older travellers, the Eurail Youth Flexi Saver, which provides 15 days of rail travel over two months in participating countries; the Eurail Flexipass First Class pass, which provides a range of options; and the Italian Flexi Railcard.

Don't forget the various bus passes including the Eurobus pass in Europe. The Eurobus began in mid-1995. It connects 19 major European cities allowing passengers to hop on and off a bus for periods of up to three months. Stops are in Austria, Belgium, the Czech Republic, France, Germany, the Netherlands, Hungary, Italy and Switzerland. Travellers under the age of 26 can purchase an unlimited two-month or three-month Eurobus pass. In the UK the Slowcoach runs one-way circuits around England, Scotland and Ireland allowing ticket holders to hop on and off the circuit as they please.

Your curriculum vitae

There has always been much debate about the value of a curriculum vitae (CV). Richard Nelson Bolles, author of *What Colour is Your Parachute?*, is very disparaging about the CV saying that it only leads to a job for about eight out of every 100 job-seekers who use it. However, for someone who is seeking a position overseas, especially a short-term position when there is not much time to network, it is essential. Another disagreement is about what a CV should look like—is one page more effective than several pages? Should a photograph be included? Should the covering letter be handwritten? In Germany, Mercedes-Benz, a company that receives piles of job enquiries and applications each year, suggests that anything longer than one page is too long. If an interview follows the CV, then this is the time to present more information.

You should organise your CV, originals of your qualifications and your references before you go. You may need to take samples of your work, and you may want to seal some documents in plastic laminate or carry them in a cardboard tube to prevent damage. Although overseas employers will not understand the intricacies of Australian or New Zealand exam scores, or the value of particular certificates, in most cases you'll be working through agencies who should know. Having your CV on disc in either Word or WordPerfect for a PC (rather than a Mac) is recommended. A bit of planning and thought about presentation of your credentials will be invaluable. You may not need them to get a job unloading trucks at four in the morning in Manchester, but it will definitely pay off if you have them handy when the need arises.

An important point needs to be made here. If you are travelling directly from home to London or another UK airport there should be no problems in carrying your CV with you if you have the appropriate visa. However, many immigration officers think that working holiday-makers should only work in a bar, so you may want to send your CV to a friend or family member, or to your post restante address, rather than carry it through immigration. If you are travelling via another country do not carry your CV or details of your work experience. A recent case in point suggests why this is downright dangerous. An Australian woman who had a UK working holiday visa in her passport decided to travel via the US to visit friends. However, her bags were searched at Los Angles and her CV was found, and she was put straight back on a plane to Australia. The US immigration officers said that the UK working holiday visa was a front and she was really wanting to find work in the US. You never win an argument with immigration officials, so don't try.

Taxation (Australia only)

One issue worth thinking about (if only because it could save you money) is your obligation to the tax collector. If you are placed overseas by a recruitment agency, consulting firm or aid organisation, your tax position should be looked after, or at least, you should be given accurate information which you can then follow up. If you are organising your own work then you will need to obtain some advice from your accountant or tax agent on your tax position. In Australia, the annual Tax Pack outlines the steps you need to go through in order to work out the tax payable on your foreign income. However, it's best to get advice on this.

Generally, the only overseas income exempt from Australian taxation is that which has been subject to a similar tax regime in the country where it was earned and is the result of 12 months of continuous work. However, where you work part of the financial year in Australia and part overseas, the overseas income will be added to what you earned in Australia for that financial year in order to establish the marginal rate at which your Australian earnings should be taxed. Some professional advice is a good idea if you intend to earn some decent money while overseas.

Clothes and packing

The principal rule for travelling is to pack light. However, if you are working you'll need to take some changes of work clothes (and maybe even a travel iron), especially if you intend working in an office.

Take clothes that are easy to look after and are versatile—the 'go anywhere' look. Lots of thin layers of clothing are easier to wear and carry than thick heavy clothes. Dark colours don't show the dirt as easily as light colours and materials that don't crush easily are recommended, especially if you intend jamming clothes into a backpack (it's best to roll them rather than lay them flat). You'll also need warm clothes if you're going to spend a winter in the UK. Remember that in mid-winter it can be dark for almost 16 hours each day and this usually means pretty dismal weather. If you're after some budget priced winter clothes in the UK try the street markets as bargains can be found. You might also find something worthwhile in the secondhand and charity shops.

Most people take a backpack of some sort and its worthwhile spending a bit more to get a decent one. It'll need to survive lots of rough handling while en route and you don't want it to slowly disassemble. If possible, find a backpack with an internal frame. These are now the most common type and have fewer external straps which can get caught in planes and trains. Better still, find one that can convert into a conventional suitcase, which is easier to carry in crowds. Take some small padlocks to lock your zippers and a small chain or similar to lock the backpack to structures to prevent it being stolen, especially at railway stations. If you do want to take a suitcase get one with wheels. Make sure all luggage is clearly labelled with your name and address.

Sex

Sex happens so it's best to be prepared. Condoms (often called durex, a brand of condoms) are available at chemists and are strongly recommended to prevent the transmission of HIV and other STDs.

Paying attention to an effective method of contraception is also worthwhile to avoid an unplanned pregnancy, which may upend your travel plans. Free condoms and contraceptive advice are available from the local Family Planning Clinic (consult the phone book for contact details) or from the Family Planning Association based at 27 Mortimer Street, London W1A 4QW. Tel: (0171) 837 5432.

Clubs

There are a number of Australasian clubs you can join to help you settle into London. One club you can join before heading off is London Orientation. There are other clubs such as Deckers you can join once you have arrived in the UK. Contact London Orientation at PO Box 241, Blackburn South Vic 3130. Tel: (03) 9894 2935. Fax: (03) 9894 2923. Website: www.ozemail.com.au/~loinfo. In New Zealand, PO Box 96 107, Auckland. Tel: (09) 358 4661.

Fax: (09) 358 0644. Email: grafton@iconz.co.nz. A membership fee (in Australia this is $65) includes an 'Off to work in the UK' pack and, upon arrival in London, a wide range of discounts, information and support to help you settle into London without hassle. You also receive help to find a job. In Australia membership is only available in conjunction with an airline booking through the Flight Centre.

Electrical appliances

The UK has a 240 V, 50 Hz standard voltage so your electrical equipment will work, although you will need an adaptor for the plug. You can find these adaptors at bookshops that have a good travel section, outdoor shops or department stores. If travelling to Europe you'll need to take some additional adaptors.

Driving

If you want to drive in the UK, for a small fee you can obtain an International Driving Permit from your local motorists' association. It's a good idea to also take your Australian or New Zealand licence. If you intend purchasing a car (not recommended even for two years given the overall cost: petrol is more than twice the price that it is in Australia) then you should also obtain a Commonwealth Motoring Conference (CMC) card which, once registered, provides the same benefits as does membership of the motorists' association at home. This reciprocal agreement, however, only lasts for one year. NRMA Travel has an excellent booklet *Overseas Motoring* which covers a range of issues related to driving overseas. Other motorists' associations should have a similar booklet.

Housekeeping

If you're going to be away for some time, don't forget to finalise things at home. Have the post office redirect your mail to an appropriate address. This doesn't cost much and it saves mail going astray. Arrange for regular accounts to be paid either directly from your bank or have a friend or family member do this for you. If you need to renew documents such as an International Driving Permit or travel insurance, make sure appropriate application forms and photocopies are left at home with someone who will do this for you. You may need to grant a power of attorney to someone and, while it may sound gruesome, writing out a will is a good idea.

The are two types of power of attorney, the general power of attorney is limited by the agreement, i.e. while you are overseas, but in any case only applies while you are mentally competent. An enduring power of attorney also applies if you become mentally incompetent such as by an accident. A recent letter from a father in the YHA's *Backpackers Essentials* recommended organising a power of attorney before travelling. In his case his son's credit card was stolen and he needed to cancel it and organise a new one. Because he did not have power of attorney the process became costly and took a lot of time. Cancel regular subscriptions such as newspapers and pay ahead for other things like insurance. Check to see that your drivers licence doesn't expire while you are overseas. If you own or rent a home or flat, notify the insurance company, as some covers are suspended if you are away for more than 60 days without telling the insurer.

A checklist of things to do and take

Six months before leaving

- ☐ Talk with others about your ideas; maybe some friends will think it's a good idea and decide to go as well.
- ☐ Sound out any contacts you may have.
- ☐ Start researching your destination and options through guide books, magazines and the Internet.
- ☐ Organise your passport.
- ☐ Keep saving!
- ☐ ....
- ☐ ....

Three months before leaving

- ☐ Check out airline prices and put down a deposit if you find something that suits you.
- ☐ Depending on your decision about airlines, take out frequent flyer membership.
- ☐ Organise credit cards, if you don't already have any.
- ☐ Talk to your bank about opening a bank account in London.
- ☐ Apply for any necessary visas.
- ☐ ....
- ☐ ....

Two months before leaving

- ☐ Check out travel insurance options.
- ☐ Visit your dentist for a check up.

- [ ] If necessary, check out vaccination requirements.
- [ ] Join the Youth Hostels Association (YHA).
- [ ] Book your accommodation.
- [ ] Organise a criminal record clearance through your local police station (for teachers and social workers).
- [ ] ....
- [ ] ....

The last month

- [ ] Visit your doctor for any necessary prescriptions or documents.
- [ ] Buy any travellers cheques (depending on the exchange rate, you might want to do this earlier).
- [ ] Photocopy tickets, insurance documents, the front page of your passport and anything else necessary (leave one copy of each with someone at home).
- [ ] Finalise your tax return, if possible.
- [ ] Organise a power of attorney and will.
- [ ] Obtain your International Driving Permit (check that your drivers licence will not expire while you are away).
- [ ] Purchase passes including transport passes and those for visiting tourist sites.
- [ ] Finalise your CV and references.
- [ ] Purchase clothes, equipment and bits and pieces (make use of YHA's membership discounts).
- [ ] Organise mail redirection and finalise rental arrangements.
- [ ] ....
- [ ] ....
- [ ] ....
- [ ] ....
- [ ] Have a party!

Organising work before you go

Bryan Havenhand

While there are extensive networks and numerous possibilities for finding work in London soon after arrival (see Chapter 15), it is also possible to organise work before leaving home. In fact, there are many agencies in Australia and New Zealand that search out as many prospective candidates as possible for positions in the UK. However, in most cases, final confirmation of a position will not be available until after an interview with the employment agency or prospective employer in the UK. This option of obtaining work before leaving home works well for those wanting a bit more surety. In addition, some of these agencies will assist in other areas such as providing advice on accommodation and help in opening a bank account.

Those with the right qualifications and experience and who are Internet savvy should be able to make contact with prospective employers over the Internet before leaving. As it is unlikely that prospective employers would be willing to deal with a potential part-time or short-term employee over the Internet, this option is most useful to those who are able to work in the UK without the constraints of the working holiday visa. That is, those people who are able to work full-time with the same employer for a lengthy period. In some cases the employer will be in a position to sponsor the applicant.

Job programs

If you would like to get a feel for what is happening in London regarding jobs and lots of other things it is possible to subscribe to publications prior to leaving. Most of the publications mentioned in this book provide for subscriptions to down-under addresses. However, *TNT Magazine* is the best value, given the cost (all are expensive), the size of the publication and amount of information in each issue. Reading *TNT* before arriving will give you a good feel for what is happening. To check the latest rates for three, six or 12 month subscriptions, write to Subscriptions, *TNT Magazine*, 14-15 Child's Place, London SW5 9RX. Fax: +44 171 341 6600. Email: enquiries@tntmag.co.uk. Website: www.tntmag.co.uk.

International Exchange Programs (IEP)

One organisation which is not an employment agency or representative but which caters for those wanting to work in the UK with a support system behind them is IEP. IEP has representation in most states including: 196 Albert Road, South Melbourne Vic 3205. Tel: (03) 9690 5890. Fax: (03) 9645 7496. Level 2/333 George Street, Sydney NSW 2000. Tel: (02) 9299 0400. Fax: (02) 9299 0399. Free call: 1300 300 912. Email: info@iep-australia.com. Webside: www.iep-australia.com. In New Zealand IEP is found at 5/120 Mayoral Drive, Auckland. Tel: (09) 366 6255. Fax: (09) 366 6156. Free call 0800 443 769. Email: info@iepnz.co.nz. Website: www.iepnz.co.nz.

IEP operates a 'Work Travel Britain' program in conjunction with BUNAC (www.bunac.org) in London, a non-profit organisation operating since 1962 and providing services to students and non-students wanting to spend time working in the UK. It is a substantial operation and last year the London office handled over 5000 participants made up of about 100 Australians, 50 New Zealanders, 4000 Americans, 1000 Canadians, 100 Jamaicans and 50 Ghanaians.

The 'Work Travel Britain' program allows participants to depart at any time throughout the year. You are responsible for obtaining your working holiday visa but for a $300 program fee, or NZ$340 for New Zealanders, you get quite a bit upon arrival in London:

- an arrival orientation in London by the UK BUNAC
- employment and accommodation listings at the BUNAC resource centres in London and Edinburgh

- BUNAC membership giving access to organised social events including weekend and day trips
- a mail holding service
- a phone message service (until you organise your accommodation)
- a free six-month National Express discount Coachcard
- a TNT London guide
- a Lonely Planet travel guide to Britain
- a *Work & Travel Britain* handbook
- a London map.

In 1996-97 52% of BUNAC participants found work within three days, 22% found work within four to six days, and 16% found work within seven to 10 days of arrival in the UK, while the remaining 10% took more than 10 days. About 15 to 20 jobs are added to the jobs' board each day. Examples of the type of work listed include: administrative assistant to architect £200 per week; waitress £200 per week; production assistant on a Macintosh computer £280 per week; English teacher £300 per week; packer £150 per week; marketing person £650 per month; bar staff £110 per week plus board; clerk in law firm £240 per week; data entry person £150 per week; coffee maker £128 per week; and computer analyst £304 per week.

The Work Experience Scheme (TWES)

Department for Education and Employment, Overseas Labour Service, W5, Moorfoot, Sheffield S1 4PQ. Website: www.open.gov.uk/dfee/ols/index.htm.

TWES provides an avenue for UK employers to employ non-UK nationals for training towards a professional or specialist qualification (the training program) or to undertake short periods of work (the work experience program). However, TWES is a difficult program to access as a UK employer must not create the positions at the expense of local employees (i.e. a TWES position must be a new position) and both the training and work experience programs are very structured. Participants in both programs are required to be over 18, and the work experience program cuts out at 35. There are many rules governing the programs which can't be listed here. Given the ability of Australians and New Zealanders to access work in the UK through the working holiday visa, this avenue is not worth pursuing unless an opportunity arises while you are in the UK. However, remember that the prospective employee is not permitted to be in the UK when the employer files the application. The work experience program is for a maximum of 12 months. It is possible to use an immigration lawyer when trying to access this scheme, but this is a substantial cost.

Student programs

Students may be able to obtain work in the UK for a limited time through exchange organisations. These include IAESTE and AIESEC.

IAESTE, PO Box 649, Hawthorn Vic 3122. Tel: (03) 9214 8577. Fax: (03) 9219 0834. Email: joconnor@swin.edu.au. Website: www.swin.edu/chem/iaeste/.

IAESTE aims to provide students at tertiary institutions with study-related technical experience overseas, including in the UK. These positions are usually available during the northern hemisphere summer (i.e. mid-year) but some are also available over the Christmas academic break. Unfortunately there is no IAESTE in New Zealand.

AIESEC, National Committee, GPO Box 3586, Sydney NSW 2001. Tel: (02) 9264 6450. Fax: (02) 9264 6067. Website: www.aiesec.org/

AIESEC, National Committee, PO Box 11-126, Manners Street, Wellington, New Zealand. Tel: (04) 499 6480. Fax: (04) 499 6488.

AIESEC runs international programs whereby students of business, economics and computing can be placed in businesses in the UK and many other countries in order to gain international experience. There are some costs associated with this scheme and it helps if you have been involved in AIESEC activities on your campus. In the first instance contact your campus business studies office or equivalent.

Recruitment agencies

There are a considerable number of agencies in Australia and New Zealand, some recruiting for specific jobs and others providing information and undertaking the early part of the recruitment process for work in the UK. Chapter 15 provides a list of contact details for some of these agencies. The occupational groups for which local recruitment is most active reflect the respective shortages in the UK. These occupational groups include teaching, information technology (a range of positions right across the industry), nursing and other medical positions, and finance, especially accountancy.

Immigration rules

Philip Trott and Peter Moss

Global mobility free of legal restraints is every traveller's ideal when it comes to travelling for the purposes of tourism or work. However, most Western countries operate a protectionist system of some sort and the UK is no exception. It is a country that has a history of excluding immigrants rather than welcoming them. With this in mind, if you wish to move as easily as possible into the UK you need to be well equipped to tackle the numerous hurdles that will face you when applying to live in the UK.

You have probably read a lot recently about changes in the UK's immigration laws following the election of a Labour Government. The biggest changes have been the abolition of the Primary Purpose Rule in marriage applications and a concession to couples who do not have the legal option of marriage. The former rule was a vicious rule designed to keep out spouses from the Indian subcontinent. In practice, it was rarely applied to the applications of spouses from Australia. The concession to couples who do not have the legal option of marriage benefits the gay partner of a resident who wants to stay in the UK following four years cohabitation.

The concession was carefully framed so that working holidaymakers can not benefit from it. Working holidaymakers are not able to live in the UK long enough to apply under this concession. The concession also does not help couples who want to stay together and who could marry but have chosen not to. It looks as if the new Government will, in general, be no more easy going in matters of immigration control than their Conservative predecessors. Indeed, Government spokespeople have recently criticised the last Government for their lack of vigour in enforcing the Immigration Rules, and the White Paper *Fairer, Faster and Firmer* (published on 27 July 1998) promises even greater powers to immigration officers.

Understanding the system

You wake up one morning with a strong urge to live in the UK, perhaps for a few years, perhaps for good. As you will need to earn your living while there, how can you satisfy this strange desire? You certainly will not fulfil your wish to emigrate to the UK by telling those nice people at the British Embassy or High Commission or on the Immigration Desk at Heathrow Airport that you feel very British and so would like to live there. The British government has a publicly declared objective of discouraging immigration for a permanent stay and confining such immigration to the close dependent relatives of persons already permanently resident in the UK.

For the past 40 years immigration to the UK has been a controversial issue. Panic over potential racial conflict, or fear of being flooded with refugees, has led to ever more restrictive immigration controls and an ever greater control over immigration from Commonwealth countries, which was unrestricted prior to 1962. On the other hand, since 1973 controls over immigration of European Union (EU) nationals and their families have been progressively abolished.

Furthermore, the EU has also entered into 'Europe Agreements' with most of the countries of Eastern Europe. These agreements confer limited rights on nationals of those countries to allow them to set up a business in the UK. As a result of these agreements, a position now exists in which, in many respects, a Polish national wishing to establish a business in the UK is likely to find it easier to achieve than would an Australian or New Zealander.

If you wish to work or set up a business in the UK you have to fit yourself into the appropriate segment of the immigration rules (currently set out in Statement of Changes in Immigration Rules HC395 as amended principally by HC26). Alternatively, you need to somehow qualify outside those rules under one of the numerous concessionary policies which the Home Office operates but which they won't always reveal.

Does your ancestry or place of birth help?

You might be a British citizen by descent and if you are, you probably already know about it. However, if you are not sure take expert advice on the matter as British nationality law is very complicated. If however you were born in the UK after 1 January 1983 this does not of itself confer British citizenship. One of your parents must be permanently resident in the UK, and it is worth noting that a father of a child born out of wedlock is excluded from the definition of 'parent' in the British Nationality Act 1981. Also, remember that although the British government permits dual citizenship, it is important to check with the authorities in your own country that any steps you take to acquire or assert your entitlement to British citizenship don't prejudice your existing citizenship.

Citizens of the EU (made up of Austria, Belgium, Denmark, France, Germany, Italy, Ireland, Finland, Sweden, Spain, the UK, Luxembourg, the Netherlands, Greece and Portugal) and citizens of the European Economic Area (EEA) (made up of Norway and Iceland) are entitled to live permanently in the UK in most circumstances, as are the non-EU or non-EEA members of their family.

There has never been any control over immigration of Irish citizens to the UK. Many Australians and New Zealanders may have Irish-born grandparents which may give rise to a claim to register as a citizen of that country.

You might therefore be able to effectively emigrate to Britain by asserting you or your spouse's entitlement to some other EU or EEA nationality. Thus, an Australian citizen with no particular claim to reside in the UK might be able to live in the UK with complete freedom to work or engage in business if he or she could prove, say, Finnish citizenship, as Finland is in the EU. All EU and EEA nationals have the right in the UK to work, set up a business, secure services or retire at any age. After four years in the UK, in any of the above capacities, the Home Office allows EU and EEA nationals to stay in the UK permanently. The nationality laws of many

European countries are extremely complicated and often in practice far less generous than they appear. Some countries appear to apply administrative delay as a means of deterring claimants to citizenship. If you think you have a claim to a nationality of an EU or EEA country it is recommended that you take expert advice.

How will having a UK-born grandparent benefit you?

This is one important opportunity open to Commonwealth citizens (and, therefore, Australians and New Zealanders), but not to others, which allows you to live and work in the UK. The rule states that Commonwealth citizens aged 17 or over may apply for entry clearance (prior consent to admission to the UK) if they can prove that one of their grandparents was born in the UK, that they are able to work and intend to take or seek employment (or self employment) and will be able to maintain and accommodate themselves without receiving state benefits. If you can show this you get permission to stay for four years with freedom to work (or be self employed) and, after this time, obtain permanent residence.

You can change from visitor to this status while in the UK. It is of course a lot simpler to resolve an immigration matter by an application to the Home Office in the UK than to pay fees for entry clearance in Canberra. However, beware if you arrive in the UK on a visit for two weeks to see your Aunt Jennifer and then the day after you arrive present a beautifully bound bundle of documents proving your descent from Arthur Bogget of Piddlehinton. You may be arrested. This is not because Bogget was one of the Tolpuddle Martyrs, and is still wanted by the Dorset magistrates, but because the Home Office may reach the (not unreasonable) conclusion that you intended to stay permanently when you came into the country the day before, and lied when you entered as a visitor. That makes you an illegal entrant.

If you seek to alter your status from visitor to a person wishing to reside in the UK by virtue of UK ancestry, do make sure that you don't find yourself locked up in one of the growing number of

Home Office detention centres housing those considered to be illegal entrants. If you are concerned about the timing of such an application, do take expert advice.

The immigration consequences of marriage

You may of course arrive with or join your British wife or husband in the UK if he or she proposes to live there permanently. Entry clearance is compulsory if you wish to secure admission on arrival as a spouse. You are expected to apply for entry clearance as a spouse in the country in which you normally live. Do not assume (as a surprisingly large number of people do) that you acquire a right of entry to the UK as a result of marriage to a British citizen. You do not. If you arrive in the UK without entry clearance while announcing an intention to join your wife or husband to live in the UK permanently, you will be refused entry.

Nothing prevents a person who is in the UK in a temporary capacity, for example as a visitor, student or working holidaymaker, from altering his or her status to that of a spouse of a British citizen who lives in the UK or a foreign national resident in the UK or, in certain circumstances, the spouse of a person working in the UK in a temporary capacity. However, beware! If you arrive on Thursday morning saying you will be in the country for two weeks, and then on Friday attend at the Home Office with a marriage certificate seeking permission to stay here permanently, you are in danger of being arrested, detained and put back on the next available plane to Australia or wherever else you came from. If you obtain entry by deception it is as if you were never given permission to enter the UK at all. You are what is called an illegal immigrant, a creature with few or no rights. So, if you do seek to alter your status from being a visitor to becoming a spouse, it is advisable to take professional advice. Timing and skill in the presentation of such applications are of the essence.

Marriage by a person who has overstayed their permission to be in the UK will not result in permission to stay being granted.

However, the Home Office will probably not enforce the departure of a person who has overstayed and whose marriage to a permanent resident settled in the UK has lasted for two years. Also, if there are any children from this marriage, it may also help prevent deportation. The special circumstances in which the Home Office will not deport married overstayers are set out in several sets of unpublished instructions which require expert interpretation. If you have overstayed your permission to stay in the UK, do not make any application to the Home Office to regularise your position without obtaining expert guidance.

Does being a fiancé or common law spouse help?

You do not actually have to marry your British 'wife' or 'husband' to gain admission to the UK. You can come to the UK as a fiancé and get married in the UK, though entry clearance as a fiancé is compulsory. You cannot, however, alter your status from that of visitor to fiancé. If you are here in a temporary capacity and want to stay here with the love of your life, then if you can legally marry, that is the only basis of stay. If you are unable to marry (for example because your partner is of the same sex), then you could qualify on the basis of the new concession to couples who cannot marry. Four years cohabitation is the basis of the requirement. The cohabitation does not have to have occurred in the UK. Entry clearance for admission in this capacity is compulsory, but you can alter your status, for example, from that of student, to the status appropriate to the new category. There is now no provision for overseas nationals who could legally marry their resident partner but who choose not to.

Spouse applications can be dealt with at the Public Enquiry Office at the Home Office, Croydon, provided that all the compulsory application forms are completed correctly, and that all the relevant evidence, including both passports, is presented.

The previous Government abolished a long standing concession by which a common law or de facto spouse was allowed to obtain entry clearance or permission to stay in the UK. The concession allowed admission or permission to remain for the common law spouse who had entered into a permanent and exclusive relationship with an EU or EEA citizen, of the opposite sex, who lived permanently in the UK. The new Government will probably re-introduce such arrangements, together with arrangements which allow well-established homosexual relationships with persons resident in the UK, to form a basis for immigration. However, at the time of writing (13 July 1997), no announcement has been made.

The current rules for working holidaymakers

Entry clearance has now become compulsory and the rather vague wording of the previous immigration rules, which reflected an easy going practice designed to welcome young Commonwealth citizens who wanted to spend extended holidays in the UK and work during that time, has been tightened up. Young Australians, New Zealanders and South Africans have probably become victims of their own popularity. UK employers like employing them and this has caused resentment in the resident labour force. The current rules are also designed to prevent working holidaymakers spinning out their stay and eventually acquiring some claim to remain in the UK permanently. The basic new requirements are that the working holidaymaker must meet the following criteria.

1) Have an entry clearance. You cannot therefore arrive in Britain and expect to be admitted as a working holidaymaker, nor can you, having been admitted as a visitor, alter your status from visitor to working holidaymaker. You have to go to a British High Commission, Consulate or Embassy (a post) overseas and apply for an entry clearance. This need not be in your home country, although not all British posts overseas deal with working holidaymaker applications; some may try to fob you off by saying that they will only deal with applications

from people who live permanently in the country in which that post is located. If you are contemplating applying for a working holidaymaker entry clearance anywhere else other than in your home country, please take professional advice.

2) Be unmarried or be married to a person who qualifies for admission as a working holidaymaker, with both husband and wife intending to take the working holiday together. Thus, there is no longer provision for a spouse to be admitted (with entry clearance) as a dependent of a working holidaymaker.

3) Be intending to take employment incidental to a holiday but not to engage in business, provide services as a professional sportsman or entertainer, or pursue a career in the UK. Some commentators have suggested that this provision confines working holidaymakers to bar work. That isn't true. Those with professional qualifications (for example, nurses) could still work as agency nurses provided they weren't going to make a career out of it in the UK and that the overall object of the trip was a holiday. If however the object is to either practice a profession or set up in business in the UK, then it is made quite clear that you can no longer use working holidaymaker status as a stepping stone.

4) Not have dependent children over five years of age or who will reach five years of age before you complete your working holiday, or have commitments which would require you to earn a regular income. The object of these provisions is probably to exclude young African Commonwealth Citizens from being working holidaymakers, but obviously all Australasians will be affected as well.

5) Not be asking for a period of permission to stay as a working holidaymaker that would make the total period in which you wished to stay as such more than two years beyond your first stay in that capacity. You cannot therefore add on the time you spent at the Munich Beer Festival to gain an aggregate period of two years as a working holidaymaker.

From this you will see that an extended holiday trip to the UK with freedom to work requires much more planning than before. If you are professionally qualified or you are contemplating establishing yourself in business, or you would like to work or intend to gain work experience to acquire a professional skill, then you should give thought to whether you qualify for admission: as a work permit holder (under either the main scheme or the training and work experience scheme); as an overseas representative to establish yourself in business or; in some other capacity under the immigration rules which allows you to work.

It has become apparent that the changes in the rules relating to working holidaymakers are accompanied by much tighter practice at the ports of entry. New written landing stamps have been prepared which restrict the working holidaymaker to specific employment incidental to the holiday. You can expect much closer questioning on arrival, or indeed on re-admission to the UK, to establish whether you still meet the requirements of the rules and whether you intend to leave at the end of your time as a working holidaymaker. It becomes more important than ever to have evidence with you on your arrival in the UK of your onward travel plans and of your savings. If you have sorted out accommodation, then have evidence of that as well.

Would you qualify for a work permit?

A work permit is an approval granted by the Department for Education and Employment (DfEE) to allow a particular employer to employ a named individual to do a specific job. Work permit holders are accorded an immigration status known as 'approved employment'. Australians, New Zealanders and South Africans are popular with UK employers because of their attitude to work and the very high standards of the qualifications which many possess in some of the professions such as teaching. Difficulties often arise because many people with such qualifications have already entered employment while in the UK as working holidaymakers and their UK employers are often anxious to retain their services. This can lead the ill-advised employer to apply for a work permit while the working holidaymaker is in the country. The application will probably be turned down by the DfEE, usually because the employer has failed to advertise the position, the job is insufficiently skilled or the qualifications which the worker has acquired have been acquired in the UK while a working holidaymaker. In any event, if the DfEE does approve the application, it is now almost certain that the Home Office will refuse that person permission to stay further. The law does not permit persons in the UK who are here as visitors or as working holidaymakers to alter their status into that of approved employment. Therefore, if you find that you receive attractive job offers while in the UK, do take professional advice before encouraging an employer to apply for a work permit on your behalf. The fact that, quite properly, the very helpful staff of the DfEE who issue work permits tell an employer that a work permit application can be made, does not mean that it should be made.

If you want to work in the UK in a full-time career post then in most circumstances, not all (you might qualify for admission as a result of your ancestry or by being an EEA national), you are going to need a work permit applied for when you are not in the UK. A UK employer applying for a work permit must normally advertise the post. The employer will need to prove that no-one resident in the UK or anywhere else in the EEA can fill that post.

However, in certain circumstances, the requirement to advertise can be dispensed with. This is normally when you are already working overseas and there is a link by way of common ownership between your existing employer and the prospective UK employer. Because of the very close links by way of common ownership between British and Australian or New Zealand and South African businesses, it can be possible to fairly easily create a situation in which an employer in the UK can transfer a worker in, for example, Australia to the UK. Care must however be taken to prove the link by way of common ownership, which is not always obvious. There are other (rare) circumstances in which the advertising requirement can be dispensed with. As a general rule, the more skilled the post and the higher the salary, the easier it will be to obtain a work permit. A work permit is also available for an individual who wishes to undergo professional training or obtain work experience in the UK.

Some work permits for so-called key workers are only available for up to three years. Therefore the successful applicant doesn't benefit from the provision by which a work permit holder with permission to stay here for four years is allowed to stay here permanently. Work permits should not be applied for at a time when the prospective worker is in the UK.

There is an exception to this in that permits for people who need training or work experience (which must be at a relatively senior level) can alter their status from being a student into being a trainee under the training and work experience scheme (TWES). There is no need for an employer to advertise to get a TWES permit, but there are strict time limits and the permit holder must leave when the permit expires. The worker in approved employment under the TWES cannot move into main scheme work permit employment.

Employers in the UK may wish to recruit Australians or New Zealanders who have recently graduated or completed training in the UK. Success is difficult with such applications. There are possible solutions, but specialist advice should always be taken in these circumstances.

Ways to work in the UK without obtaining a work permit

1) Establish yourself in business. You can come to the UK to set up a business or as a business investor. However, this requires a very large capital investment and is hedged with other restrictions which make it an expensive and rather tedious way of emigrating to the UK. As a result of agreements between the EU and various Eastern European countries, the capital requirement does not apply to citizens of these countries who wish to establish themselves in business in the UK.

2) Acting as a sole representative. There is also a facility for senior employees of overseas companies which have no branch or subsidiary in the UK to live in the UK having obtained entry clearance to represent that company. The rules in relation to overseas representatives have been tightened recently. In particular, there is a new requirement that the worker must have been recruited overseas.

Great skill is required in the successful preparation and presentation of an application, either for a businessperson or for an overseas representative, and you should not contemplate an application in either of these capacities without seeking professional advice. There can be a very great delay in the processing of such applications, which should never be contemplated without a thorough consideration of practical alternative applications, perhaps involving the work permit route.

3) Writers or artists. Writers, composers and artists may apply for entry clearance outside the UK to come to the UK as self-employed persons in those capacities. Regrettably, however, the rules no longer encourage young people with perhaps limited means but with lots of potential talent to apply to live in the UK to establish themselves in that capacity.

The current requirement is that the applicant must 'have established himself outside the UK as a writer, composer or artist, primarily engaged in producing original art which has been published (other than exclusively in newspapers or magazines), performed or exhibited for its literary, musical or artistic merit and has for the preceding year been able to maintain and accommodate himself and any dependents from his own resources without working except as a writer, composer or artist and will be able to maintain and accommodate himself and any dependents from his own resources without working except as a writer, composer or artist and without recourse to public funds.' These changes are to be regretted in that they deny opportunities that were open to young people of talent to develop their artistic careers.

Studying

Coming to study in the UK is expensive and overseas student fees (which will apply to you) are considerably higher than those charged to residents and EU and EEA nationals. The student must be engaged in 15 hours per week of organised daytime study, or be attending a degree course at a publicly funded university, must be able to pay for his or her studies and must be able to persuade the immigration authorities that he or she intends to leave on completion of his or her studies.

A student may enter the UK without having obtained entry clearance as a student, but if you propose to embark on a lengthy course of study in the UK without having obtained entry clearance, it will be highly desirable for you to bring evidence of enrolment and of the very substantial financial resources that will be needed to pay for the course. The student has to be able to support and maintain himself or herself without working. Having obtained permission to stay as a student, it is possible to obtain permission from the Department of Employment to take part-time work, provided it does not interfere with your studies, or undertake a one-off three month internship with an international company in the long vacation.

Getting permission to stay permanently in the UK as a result of long residence

The Home Office accepts that persons who have lived in the UK lawfully for 10 years have become established and will normally allow such persons to stay permanently. This concession outside the immigration rules is well established and publicly announced in Parliament. Remember that 10 years does mean 10 years and, in theory, the 10 years has to be spent continuously in the UK, although, in practice, a certain amount of leeway is allowed. A half-baked 10 year rule application may do enormous harm to your prospects of remaining in some other capacity, e.g. as a student.

If you are in the UK having overstayed your permission to remain and no Deportation Order has been made against you, and you are of good character, then at the exercise of their discretion the Home Office will probably allow you to remain in the UK if you have been there for 14 years. However, do take professional advice if contemplating making an application based on long residence.

Professional advice on immigration matters

This advice is available from solicitors, Citizens Advice Bureaux and voluntary bodies such as the Immigrants Advisory Service (IAS) and the Joint Council for the Welfare of Immigrants (JCWI), and from immigration consultants. Most reputable solicitors with a substantial immigration practice are members of the Immigration Law Practitioners Association (ILPA). Consultants are unregulated and are of variable quality. Also, immigration consultants are not able to advise the very poor under the Green Form Legal Advice and Assistance Scheme. The government is considering introducing licensing for immigration consultants, but until this happens, you are strongly advised to avoid using the services of immigration consultants, and to be careful as to which solicitor you choose for immigration advice.

The key to success with the UK immigration authorities is to know firstly what you want to achieve, secondly what the law requires, and thirdly to present yourself with supporting documentation in such a way that the appropriate official will be able to place you in the appropriate category, either within or outside the immigration rules, and therefore give you what you want: entry or permission to stay in the UK.

Immigration law is often complicated and difficult to find. Specialist legal advice is not cheap but getting the right advice is a good investment.

Philip Trott and Peter Moss can be contacted at: Bates, Wells & Braithwaite Solicitors, Cheapside House, 138 Cheapside, London EC2V 6BB. Tel: (0171) 551 7777. Fax: (0171) 551 7800.

My advice

Belinda Cranston

To have studied London to the full is to know that London tells her own story, and that no one can tell it for her. Whatever credit may come to those who act as scribe, it is after all a small thing, for the inspiration is drawn from the great city itself. Sir Lawrence Gomme

The widely held stereotype of London being a damp, grey and miserable experience need not ring true, and is certainly not mentioned amongst these words uttered by the late Sir Lawrence Gomme.

However, in considering when to go to London, bear in mind that throughout the English summer, the sun can rise as early as 5.00am and set as late as 10.30pm. This allows the months of June, July and August to be more welcoming for the newly arrived antipodean than November and December, when short, cold days can be quite discouraging.

Preparing to go

Unless you are able to command the salary of a chartered accountant, I would recommend having access to at least $10,000 if you plan to stay in the UK for up to a year or more. This will be of assistance in allowing you to enjoy the rich diversity of social and cultural opportunities which London and the UK have to offer. I always found it a shame to meet antipodean travellers who felt they could not go anywhere or do anything in London, let alone in Europe, because they scraped past UK immigration officers with the minimum $3000 required to prove they could temporarily support themselves.

To accomplish the difficult task of opening a bank account in the UK, I would recommend obtaining a reference letter from your bank manager in Australia or New Zealand before leaving home. Unfortunately, foreigners are regarded with caution by English bank managers, and in order to open an account, are sometimes requested to have unlikely documents such as a utility bill in their name for proof of residence in the UK.

As far as clothing goes, thermal underwear will never go astray. If you plan on working in an office it is also a good idea to pack some appropriate office attire. While a warm coat is a must, this sort of thing is bulky to pack. For this reason it is probably just as easy to purchase a coat of high quality from a London market at a price much cheaper than you would expect to pay in Australia or New Zealand. Try the markets at Leather Lane, EC1 or Petticoat Lane, E1.

If you can't get a copy of a *London A-Z* street directory before you depart Australia, try to obtain one as soon as you arrive. I referred to it almost every day while living in London, and always kept a copy in my handbag.

Arriving

Short-term accommodation

If you already have friends living in the UK, then its great to be able to land on them when you first arrive. Bear in mind however that Australians have a reputation for taking advantage of other people's hospitality by overstaying their welcome on sofas and on living room floors. While you can probably get away with staying at the home of a close relative for quite some time, it is best not to impose on friends for any longer than say, two weeks. This is unless you can agree on a mutual arrangement. For those of you who do not know anyone to land on immediately, there is an abundant choice of hostels and hotels. I found the Porchester Hotel in Prince's Square, Bayswater W2, ideal: it is clean, modern, friendly, serves breakfast and allows you to pay a weekly rate of £70, which is relatively cheap compared with the nightly rate of £19.

Long-term accommodation

Pick up a free copy of *TNT Magazine* from major London Underground and British rail stations to find a list of antipodean households you can join from around £50-70 per week. These are great places to meet people and establish contact with future travel companions, although the cheap rent might mean you'll end up further from the heart of London than you'd planned, for example, in Willesden Green, Kensal Green, Shepherd's Bush or Acton. Try to get a copy of *TNT Magazine* on a Monday, the day it comes out, as vacant rooms in well sought after locations are in high demand.

If it's English people rather than antipodeans you would prefer to live with, try looking in *LOOT*, a newspaper which you can pick up from most newsagents.

'Home share' is another option for those seeking long-term accommodation. This arrangement is ideal for those who do not want to spend their hard-earned money on rent as accommodation is exchanged for assisting an elderly person with meals and light duties around the house. You are also expected to provide companionship. Although you might only spend around ten hours a week helping out where needed, most arrangements will require you to spend each night at your home sharer's residence. This is not to say that your social life will go out the window, but when you do want to go out it's polite to give your home sharer advanced notice.

Home share works well for some people, although obviously some personality combinations work better than others. I was placed with a former MP and his wife in a five-storey terrace in Pimlico. It was a difficult situation with the class conscious 'Lady' of the house regularly quizzing me on my family background and complaining of my 'refusal' to let go of my Australian accent. As well as needing to adopt an English accent, I was also advised to fold bed linen neatly and precisely before it was placed in the washing machine. The rationale behind this task was to make the job of ironing the linen after it was washed easier. Since I am not the type to iron linen after it is washed I found the whole procedure rather tedious. I stayed on for just six weeks, although an easy going and tolerant friend of mine did not mind staying with her home sharer for six months. For successful arrangements to take place, a lot depends on personalities being compatible as well as a flexible approach from both parties. Previous experience in a similar situation is also an advantage. If interested, *TNT Magazine* regularly advertises opportunities in the accommodation section.

Employment

TNT Magazine is again a good place to start when seeking employment. If you already have friends living in London, ask them to send copies of the employment pages to you before you leave Australia. Alternatively you can ask to have the whole magazine sent but this results in the cost of postage being expensive.

A wide diversity of employment opportunities is available. You could find yourself joining the crew of a hot air balloon, working as a receptionist in a luxury hotel in Chelsea, or sampling the life of the British aristocracy by working as a chamber maid in a Cotswolds mansion. While waitressing and bar work will earn you only just enough to cover basic living costs, teachers, administrative staff and those working in medical fields are paid quite well. The real winners are chartered accountants, who can command £20-30 per hour. Partly qualified accountants are paid around £15-20 per hour while account assistants and secretaries earn about £7-10 per hour.

With as much as 70% of London's temporary office market comprising Australians, New Zealanders and South Africans, competition from financial recruitment agencies for the attention of these travellers is intense. Some agencies offer 'free weekends away' for new recruits who have worked just one week. Others are astute enough to meet antipodean travellers at Heathrow airport immediately after their passports are stamped with right of entry declarations. If you are registered with several agencies, it is possible that a rival agency to the one you obtain a job through will attempt to poach you by offering a higher hourly rate than you are already earning.

Many people find temping in London advantageous to their careers. Anna, a thirty-year-old product accountant from Melbourne believes that because Australians have a good reputation in London, it makes it easy for those new arrivals to pick up work. Now based in London and managing the customer accounting division of a multi-national gas company, she says 'different approaches in accounting are used in London, enabling one to adopt a wider perspective and to use different methodologies to find work'.

For travellers on a two-year UK working holiday visa it is important to remember that you are not entitled to '... enter employment paid or unpaid other than as a working holiday-maker ...' and that you do not '... engage in any business or profession without the consent of the Secretary of State of the Home Department'. You should also bear in mind that working holiday visas are issued on the condition that individuals will only work for half the length of time they spend in the UK. While in the past travellers have been able to turn a blind eye to this restriction, recruitment agencies are now audited on the length of time that their Australian and New Zealand candidates spend in the UK workforce. When immigration officials discover that an individual has worked beyond the allowed length of time stated on their visa, both the agency and the individual are fined.

As a rule, it is best not to stay with any one employer for longer than three months. It is also a good idea to 'collect' a few stamps in your passport soon after you depart Australia. I heard of an instance where an Australian traveller on a working holiday visa remained in London for sixteen months before she went to Amsterdam for a long weekend. As it was the first time she had gone to Europe, she aroused the suspicion of immigration officers at Heathrow airport immediately. They questioned her at length regarding the amount of time she had spent working in London. She wasn't put on the next flight back to Australia but was extremely distressed.

Recreation

Going out in London need not always cost a fortune. A highlight during my first month of arriving was watching Pat Cash and Mary Pierce play a mixed doubles match at Wimbledon on the Centre Court. The ticket cost only £6 because it was 'second hand'. These tickets are originally purchased at the start of the day for around £36. If purchasers do not wish to remain at

Wimbledon for the whole day, they are requested to return the ticket when they leave. The ticket is then resold and proceeds are given to a charity. To obtain one of these tickets it is best to arrive at Wimbledon after 4.00pm.

It is also possible to purchase cheap tickets for the 'BBC proms' by showing up a couple of hours earlier than the scheduled time and queuing for a 'standing room' ticket. These are available throughout the English summer for as little as £2 each and enable you to listen to some spectacular performances. Check newspapers for program guides.

If it's the Queen you would like to see, go along to Australia House on the Strand to pick up an application form to attend one of her annual summer garden parties.

To obtain an up-to-date guide to London's clubs, theatres, restaurants, cultural and recreational activities, pick up a copy of *Time Out*. This magazine is published weekly and is available from newsagents.

You can never be stuck for something to do while living in London. Make the most of opportunities by being aware of what is going on around you. If you are invited to something that would not normally interest you, go along anyway. It's all part of the experience.

Meeting English people

While they may seem conservative, self-conscious and even 'stand-offish' on the surface, the English can also be described as quirky, tactful, sharp-witted and, contrary to what you might expect, will quite happily 'drink you under the table' at a moments notice.

Don't assume to bond as quickly with the English as you might with Australians and New Zealanders while in London. A lack of inhibition from Australians, in particular, can be easily mistaken for rudeness. While they are well liked for being fun, lively, assertive, friendly, unpretentious and adventurous, the English might also feel Australians are 'in your face'.

Be patient when getting to know the English. Once you get beneath that reserved exterior, you'll have a friend for life.

First things first

Bryan Havenhand

If you're flying into London you'll almost certainly arrive at either Heathrow Airport or Gatwick Airport. These airports are where London starts for the international traveller. Forget Mascot, Tullamarine and Auckland airports, Heathrow is the busiest airport in Europe and Gatwick is the busiest single runway airport in the world. Both of these airports handle over 20 million passengers each year. If you haven't been to Europe before (or large North American or Asian cities) then your definition of big cities is about to be revised. Even though both these airports work well and cater to a vast number of people each day, you won't have to do battle with the entire airport complex upon arrival. The Australian High Commission warns travellers to be aware of thieves at major railway stations and airports as there have been many reports of stolen luggage. Keep a sharp eye on your possessions at all times. There is also an increasing number of reports of pickpockets at work on London's Underground.

Passing through immigration and customs

Remember that even though you have a visa or permit stamped in your passport (unless you possess a British passport or that of another European Union country), the final say on whether you can enter the UK rests with the immigration officer on duty. This means you should be smartly dressed, and able to readily prove that you are meeting the requirements of your visa, particularly in terms of how much money you will have access to in the UK. You may also need to show your return ticket, so have this handy.

Once through immigration, collect your bags and proceed through customs, which in the UK is an honour system. There are two outlets, green and red. Green is for 'nothing to declare' and red is for those with 'something to declare'. If you are not sure you may choose to go to the red outlet and ask, but you will automatically get a bag search. There are random searches on the green outlet so be sure of what you are carrying.

Arriving at Heathrow Airport

Although Heathrow is an extremely busy airport, it was recently voted the second best in Europe by frequent travellers and first in a number of other categories such as safety, customs clearance, incoming passport control and duty free shopping. Still the accolades are probably not enough to make you want to hang around too long.

Heathrow has four terminals and if you are flying Qantas you'll arrive at terminal four but you might find yourself arriving at one of the other terminals, i.e. one, two or three. All terminals are serviced equally well. If you are planning to meet someone at the airport on arrival make sure you get very specific instructions as to where to meet them. Preferably get a map from the person you are intending to meet (and a phone number if possible). You won't feel like wandering around trying to find someone after a long flight from down-under. If you do get lost the information desk staff are very helpful. There are four options for getting into central London.

Heathrow Express

The recently opened Heathrow Express train will take you the 17 miles from Heathrow to Paddington Station in 15 minutes. Run by BAA, it cost about £450 million to build and is expected to carry six million passengers a year which supposedly will remove 3000 cars from the road to Heathrow each day. There is plenty of room on board and a one-way fare will cost either £10 or £20 for first class (not worth it as you are only on the train for 15 minutes). Given that you will be feeling pretty jaded (assuming you have flown from home in one go) this train is recommended. Once you arrive at Paddington Station you will be able to catch an Underground train, a bus or taxi—follow the signs or ask for directions.

Underground

Catching the Underground from Heathrow Airport costs less (a one-way ticket is about £3.50) but it takes 45 minutes to get to Paddington Station, which is bad news if you have plenty of luggage, particularly if you are boarding the train during peak times (when the trip will take longer than an hour). Your bulky luggage will not be greeted with enthusiasm on a crowded train. In fact, every now and then there is a public debate in London as to whether backpacks should be allowed on the Underground at all. If you have purchased a Visitor Travelcard before leaving home then you can use this to catch a train from Heathrow. When getting out at your destination be aware that some Underground stations, especially those in central London, have several outlets. Bank for example, has nine. Make sure you know which one to take.

Bus

The Airbus runs from Heathrow to central London and it is your typical red double-decker London bus. The Airbus leaves every 15 to 30 minutes depending on the time of day, and costs around £7 one-way. It leaves from outside all Heathrow terminals so follow the signs or ask at the information desk. There are two routes: A1 goes to Victoria Station and A2's destination is Kings Cross Station. Work out which one suits you best. You can use your Visitor Travelcard on this bus as well. The advantage of the bus is that you get to see London on the way in.

Taxi

This is the most expensive option if you are travelling by yourself and going into central London—over £40. However, if there are three or four travelling together or if you are going elsewhere in London then it may be feasible. A minicab will cost about £25 but agree on a fare before you get in because minicabs have no meters. A trip into central London can take up to one hour, depending on the traffic.

Arriving at Gatwick Airport

Gatwick is smaller in size than Heathrow but not far behind in passenger numbers. It is further outside London to the south, but like Heathrow Airport there are a number of options for travelling to central London.

Gatwick Express

The Gatwick Express runs non-stop and departs Gatwick every 15 minutes for Victoria Station. The trip takes about 30 minutes. Once in the Gatwick Arrivals Hall follow the signs to the Gatwick Express. You can purchase a ticket on board the train or at the station. More information is available at www.gatwickexpress.co.uk.

Connex South Central

This train is one of the 25 privatised parts of the old British Rail. It runs every 15 minutes during the day and every hour at night. The cost is about £8.50 one-way to Victoria Station in central London where you can join the Underground system, catch a bus or taxi.

Flightline

Flightline is the bus service from Gatwick to London. It has several stops en route to Victoria Station in central London. More details are available from www.speedlink.co.uk.

Getting to your accommodation

It is strongly recommended that you have pre-booked accommodation. You should also have the name of the nearest Underground station or bus route and stop number. If the agent from whom you are intending to purchase the accommodation can't give you this information then find one who can. The big advantages of pre-booked accommodation are that it will cost less and take away the stress of having to find a roof over your head on arrival so that you can sleep off your jet lag.

Contacting home

Once you find your accommodation you might want to make a quick call home. You'll be able to use the phone card you brought with you or use your mobile (remembering that the mobile will be a lot more expensive.) If you're stuck, Australians can always use Telstra's reverse charge facility with Australia Direct by phoning 0800 856 6161. Remember the time difference and don't forget about the impact of daylight saving in both countries: New Zealand is +12 hours, EST is +10 hours, CST is +9.5 hours and WST is +8 hours.

There are plenty of cybercafes around if you'd rather send an email. *TNT Magazine* prints a list of these each week and you can check TNT's website at www.tntmag.co.uk for an up-to-date list. Expect to pay about £6 per hour at most cybercafes, though some charge £1.50 for 10 minutes. There are various sliding scales for charges but the market is fairly competitive.

Sending a fax via the post office can break the bank. If you are staying at or near Earls Court you'll find Motto by turning right when you come out of the Earls Court Underground onto Earls Court Road. Motto sells a decent coffee in addition to offering an international phone service, which is claimed to be the cheapest in Earls Court, along with a fax service that charges 99p for the first page and 25p for each subsequent page. Other such outlets can be found in different parts of London that have a high transcient population.

Finding your way around

If you don't already have a copy you should get hold of a *London A-Z*—just about everyone in London has a copy—and similar guides are simply referred to as 'an A-Z'. You can find one at a newsagent; they range from pocket-size upwards and begin at about £3. Have a look at the different versions and pick one that will meet your needs. If you are in another city an equivalent street directory will exist.

Getting around

You should have a Visitor Travelcard with you, which you purchased at home, so use it to get to your accommodation and continue to use it until it expires. You'll then need to organise a Travelcard of which there are a great many variations. Pick up information from a London Transport office or just about any Underground station. It's best to start with a weekly ticket because it's a heck of a lot cheaper than daily tickets and means you can move faster through the system, especially at peak hour (as you won't have to queue for a ticket). A weekly ticket for Zones 1 and 2 will cost £16.30 and this will cover the Underground, bus and local rail. A daily ticket will cost £3.50. You'll need a passport-sized photo for the weekly ticket, which will come with a map, a ticket holder and other bits and pieces.

A taste of London

Courtesy YHA UK

'When a man is tired of London, he is tired of life'. So wrote Dr Johnson in 1773. If he were around today, the learned lexicographer would be having an absolute ball. Cool Britannia or not, the capital is one place that never goes out of fashion.

As the levels of PMT—that's pre-millennial tension—begin to rise, and the city prepares itself for the greatest show on earth, now would seem a great time to dive into London. You might not bump into the latest Pearly King and Queen, aka Liam and Patsy, but London in the naughty 90s is home to far more than just one musical oasis. Whether you're a 70s retrohead, a drum 'n' bass freak, or into Latin jazz or hip-hop, the streets of London are definitely paved with gold.

Back in the swinging 60s, the London scene positively exploded, capturing the feverish imagination of an entire generation the world over. Mary Quant was going down a storm on Carnaby Street, Marianne Faithfull and Mick Jagger were getting into mischief at the Great Marlborough Street magistrates court, and Jimi Hendrix was setting fire to guitars as if there were no tomorrow. London continues to set a furious pace dictated by the likes of art terrorist Damien Hirst, Britpop novelists Nick Hornby and Helen Fielding, and a host of waifish supermodels known simply as Kate, Jodie or Stella.

It would be easy to come to London and spend your time seeing the sights that are so quintessentially English: the changing of the guard at Buckingham Place, the Tower of London's flamboyant yeomen warders, and Westminster Abbey. But much of London's charm comes from its desire to always be one step ahead of itself, to preside forever over the cutting edge of cool. Some of the capital's efforts may at first be dubbed ridiculous by the pundits but, sooner or later, even the silliest of trends catches on – remember punk or even the New Romantics? So, hanging out in an arty Notting Hill cafe all afternoon or doing the rounds in Soho's chic bohemian bars is as good a way as any to see what makes London, and Londoners, tick. And if you do happen to find, heaven forbid, that the English live up to their reputation for being reserved and inscrutable, you can always take time-out in one of the many watering holes that double as an Australian or New Zealand home from home. Try the Walkabout Inn in Covent Garden or half the pubs around Acton!

Then again, you might be pleasantly surprised by the distinct change in temperature amongst Londoners. Gone is the stiff upper lip, the sniffy sangfroid. In these post-Diana days, everybody wants to be all touchy-feely instead. We've got New Labour, so why not New London too?

For a taste of real London, spend a bit of time doing exactly what its residents do. Catch some top-of-the-league football by watching Arsenal play at Highbury. Hop along to the free Try-Out night at Covent Garden's Comedy Cafe on a Wednesday evening when hapless wannabe comics run through their act as fire-eaters, mime artists and street musicians all do their thing.

As a year-round city, London always seems to be buzzing. November plays host to the hugely successful London Film Festival. December is a month-long party in the run-up to Christmas, and New Year can only be described as mad. During the summer months, the action moves to the great outdoors. Time your trip to coincide with the August bank holiday weekend when Britain's biggest and wildest open-air party, the Notting Hill Carnival, which celebrates London's Caribbean community and culture, brings London to a standstill. From steel bands to the very hottest sounds from Jamaica's dance halls, this is a two-day extravaganza that will have you pleading for mercy by the end of it. Other annual events to look out for include Pride, one of the world's largest gay festivals, usually held in July, and the June Fleadh in Finsbury Park, a rip-roaring celebration of Irish music. Or maybe you just want to sit by the river and watch the world go past. Whatever the next century holds, you can be sure that London is one place where the future looks rosy.

Accommodation

Bryan Havenhand

If you are without relatives or friends who are able to offer a floor or better upon arrival in London, it is highly recommended that you pre-book your accommodation, at least for one if not two weeks. The good thing about booking ahead is that when you finally escape the airport, you have somewhere to go. It beats that 'Now what do I do' feeling. If you don't like the accommodation you've pre-booked you'll have no difficulty moving on to something better.

When it comes to accommodation the main shock for antipodeans is the cost, especially when what you end up with is not all that great. London is significantly more expensive than the rest of the UK. In July 1998 the average London house price was £108,019 while the average price for the UK overall was £71,765. This explains the high cost of accommodation in London but also illustrates the wealth difference between London and the rest of the country, especially areas to the north. The region with the lowest average price for a house, not surprisingly, was northern England at £52,325. The average for Scotland was £60,054 while in the South East of England, as affluent an area as London, the average price for a house was £98,181.

If you are going to be living and working outside of London then the process of finding accommodation is similar to that outlined here. There is bound to be a YHA hostel in the medium sized or bigger UK cities or, in the unlikely situation that you are heading to a smallish place, a B&B will be available. The cost of renting will be less than in London as indicated (roughly) by the house prices given above. The local Travel Information Centre will be able to assist in finding accommodation. If your travel agent is not able to direct you to the local Travel Information Centre then the British Tourist Authority (BTA) will be able to. In Australia telephone the BTA on (02) 9377 4400 and in New Zealand telephone (09) 303 1446.

Pre-booked accommodation

Organising two weeks of pre-booked accommodation—which will usually be cheaper than paying for it in London—is not being overcautious. By the time you have your feet on the ground, have done a bit of sightseeing and have orientated yourself and begun to look for work, two weeks will have passed without effort. Don't underestimate the time it takes to get around London, it's a big city, especially when you are not familiar with its 'ins and outs'. If you will be arriving during summer then it is imperative that you book ahead. If you are arriving in July or August, both peak tourist months, this means booking a month or more before you leave.

If you are a member of the YHA you can use YHA's International Booking Network to book up to six months in advance. Alternatively, you might pre-book accommodation in something other than a youth hostel if your travel agent has a special deal going. Depending on the time of year you are arriving in London, you may be able to pre-book accommodation directly via telephone, fax or the Internet. Some hostels and hotels are not too interested in taking extended bookings from individuals somewhere in the Southern Hemisphere in the middle of summer when they can be almost guaranteed a full house at a higher per night charge from the multitudes of tourists already in London.

Short-term accommodation options

There are many options for shorter term accommodation and some of these may be suitable for longer term stays as well. The great advantage of staying in hostels over, say, B&Bs is that you get to meet lots of others who are travelling or working in the UK. Establishing a network of friends and acquaintances early will also help blow away those homesick blues.

YHA hostels

There are seven YHA hostels in London: City of London, Earls Court, Hampstead Heath, Highgate Village, Holland House, Oxford

Street and Rotherhithe. There is something going for each of these hostels whether it is price, location, facilities or the size of the dorms. Prices vary from about £12 to about £22 per night. There are 240 hostels throughout England and Wales and 80 in Scotland. Check your YHA UK hostel guide or contact the YHA office for the latest details. There are no age limits for guests.

Independent hostels

There are many of these scattered around inner London and other major cities of the UK. These hostels do not have membership requirements and there are few rules. However, compared to YHA hostels the independents are usually cheaper but the accommodation is not as comprehensive or as well maintained as YHA establishments.

Earls Court is still a favourite haunt for those from down-under given the great number of budget hostels and hotels within a short walking distance of the Earls Court Underground. However, Earls Court is not what it used to be and is rather down at the heels these days with a limited choice for eating out or stocking up the larder. Still, there are lots of backpackers there and it is a good place to meet others, so you might want to move there after your initial accommodation booking has expired. Expect a dorm bed to start at around £10-12 per night while a single room will start at about £20 per night. Weekly rates will usually be cheaper. Check to see if breakfast is included.

Bed and Breakfasts

B&Bs can be civilised and homely forms of accommodation, though establishments will vary considerably in ambience, facilities and price. The main drawback is that you are not going to meet as many people as you would staying in hostels and hotels. Prices for single rooms start from around £15 per night and this should include breakfast; double rooms should be about twice this price. Further from central London you'll find B&Bs that offer weekly and monthly rates that are quite a discount on daily rates but may be a bit difficult to reach by public transport at night.

University and college accommodation

If you arrive during university and college academic breaks then student accommodation can be a good deal. Apart from Christmas and Easter the main period of availability is from the end of June to mid-September. For my last trip to London I was able to book a room—by fax from home—at the new Great Dover Street residences of Kings College London for about £11 per night (without breakfast). The residence was new so although the room was small it was self-contained with a bathroom and fridge. The kitchen was shared between six rooms though you rarely saw the other residents.

Camping

If you're keen on camping and want serious low cost accommodation then there are some London camping options available. However, if you're planning to roll up for work in the morning looking spic and span, camping out is not a good option, and London's weather can be pretty miserable. There is Tent City at Old Oak Common Lane W3 with the nearest station being East Acton. It is open from June to September and beds in dormitory tents will cost about £7 per night. There is limited space for individual tents. You should book in advance on (0181) 743 5708. Another Tent City is found at Millfields Road, Hackney with the nearest station being Clapton. There is space for tents here for about £5 per night. Book on (0181) 985 7656. Alternatively, try Lee Valley Park at Picketts Lock Lane, Edmonton N9. The nearest station is Tottenham Hale from which it is necessary to catch a bus. This site is open all year round and charges are about £5 per person per night and about £2.50 for electricity.

Squatting

An even cheaper option is squatting. While squatting itself is not illegal, breaking and entering is. There are some long-term squats in abandoned buildings, but as you could imagine conditions are fairly basic. You'll discover information on this in London but don't attempt it until you have made contact with the Advisory

Service for Squatters, 2 St Pauls Road, London N1. Tel: (0171) 359 8814. They publish *The Squatters' Handbook* for about £1.

Longer term accommodation options

The cost of accommodation in London means that most people end up sharing, even if it is only the bathroom. To rent your own self-contained flat, even a one-bedroom flat, requires a significant regular salary. In any case, living by yourself means you are less likely to meet others, either temporary residents or the genuine local. However, London is set up for renting and, unlike at home, you don't need to cart your linen and pots and pans with you as these are mostly laid on. If you would like some advice on rental issues check with the local Citizen's Advice Bureau. Women's Link provides free advice for women on a range of issues including accommodation. They are located at 8-9 Giltspur Street, London EC1A 9DE. Tel: (0171) 248 1200. Fax: (0171) 248 1570.

YWCA and YMCA hotels

Don't overlook the Young Women's Christian Association (YWCA) and the Young Men's Christian Association (YMCA) hotels. These tend to cater for the longer term resident and usually need to be booked well in advance. Membership of the YWCA is $20 and the cost of the directory is $5. For more details telephone the Australian YWCA head office in Melbourne on (03) 9329 5188 or in New Zealand contact the YWCA in Auckland on (09) 377 8763. Not known to many people is that men are allowed to stay in most YWCA hotels. The YMCA also has a worldwide directory for $15 and membership is $15, though you don't need to be a member to stay at a YMCA hotel. For more details telephone the Australian YMCA head office in Melbourne on (03) 9699 7655 or in New Zealand contact the head office in Auckland on (09) 303 2068. There are two YWCA and 10 YMCA hotels in or near central London.

Bedsits

Bedsits are the next up from B&Bs and are usually self-contained rooms that include a bed and pixi-sized kitchen with stove, fridge and sink/hand basin. The bathroom facilities are normally shared with other residents in the building. Some bedsits also share a kitchen which may not be as clean as you would like. Bedsits are the cheapest way to get into renting as up-front costs are less than renting a flat or house and you are not committed to a minimum stay of several months. Bedsit rents start at around £50-60 per week and go up from there depending on the location, condition and facilities of the bedsit. You will usually be required to feed the meter with coins to keep the electricity coming, though hot water and gas are covered by your rent. Don't be afraid to do a thorough inspection before signing up so you can check the condition and ambience of the place—some can be pretty awful. Check the condition and cost of the room heating so you can factor this into your rental cost. You should also check the security of the area and the building, and how far it is from public transport, including any Night Bus services. Try to meet some residents.

Studios, shared flats and houses

Studios are a mini-flat of sorts with your own bathroom and kitchen facilities and are often split level with your own entrance to the street, though these days only one of these characteristics is usually present. Rent is from £80-90 per week. Renting a room in a shared flat or house can cost anything from about £40-50 per week (plus bills) depending on the location and condition of the flat. The big advantage of sharing in London, like anywhere, is that you are likely to meet a lot more people than having a room by yourself. This is handy if you are looking for travelling companions later on.

The easiest entry point for renting is to simply answer a 'wanted' ad seeking someone to share an existing rental arrangement. If wanting to set up your own rental arrangement, the up-front cost will usually be high, especially if you are signing the lease. In this case, you'll probably be asked for a six or 12-month lease, a months rent in advance and another months rent as a bond against damage.

Before committing yourself to any renting arrangement find out who pays the electricity, gas, water and phone. Make sure there are no outstanding amounts owing on these utilities; occasionally short-term residents do a runner and leave the mess for someone else. Remember to ask:

- in who's name are the utility accounts
- who pays the for the TV licence (about £80 for a colour set)
- who pays the Council tax, how much it is and when it is due
- what the arrangements are if something needs repair and who pays for it
- and, if you are moving into an existing rental arrangement, how the house cleaning and food supply are organised and whether or not having friends stay overnight is a problem.

Finding longer term accommodation

First you need to be sure of where you want to live and this will often depend on where you work and your hours of work. When you find something that looks right you need to get in early as good places can be snapped up quickly. Accommodation is cheaper further from central London but remember to factor in the cost of transport as well as the frequency of trains and trams outside of business hours—a late night on the town can be a hassle if there is infrequent transport home. Except for the London Underground all trains in the UK are now privatised and some services to more distant suburbs have acquired a reputation for unreliable service after peak hours.

Many magazines and newspapers will carry ads for flats, houses or share accommodation. Try *Loot*, *The Evening Standard* and *TNT Magazine*. *Loot* comes out five times a week and is available in most newsagents for about £1.30. It includes a rental section as well as job vacancies. The ads are free so you are able to use it to place an ad to find accommodation in particular areas. *The Evening Standard* is a London only newspaper with plenty of rental and employment ads. *TNT Magazine* is free, much sort after and comes out every Monday. It can be found in special bins outside tube stations, some travel agents and high traffic areas in central London. Be quick to get your copy. It includes a rental section which lists a range of share accommodation options including flats, houses, studios, bedsits and rooms for rent.

Other publications with a small rental section include *Southern Cross* and *New Zealand News UK*, both of which come out on a Wednesday, and the *London Visitors' Guide* produced by Time Out is available in newsagents for about £4. It has a good list across a range of prices. *Time Out* comes out mid-week and includes a property section in the classifieds.

Capital Radio, 30 Leicester Square WC2, produces a flat share list which is available at 4pm every Friday, but this is a popular list and the best places go quickly. You'll also find this list in Saturday's 'Guardian Guide' in the *Guardian* newspaper.

You're more likely to find Aussie and Kiwi group houses in the Australasian press and Brits wanting a flatmate in the mainstream press and *Loot*. Alternatively, you can pay a real estate agent in the area you are interested in moving to a fee to chase up accommodation that suits your requirements. This should cost about £50. The Jenny Jones Agency at 40 South Molton Street, London W1, Tel: (0171) 493 4801, provides this service free.

A guide to London suburbs

The following is a light-hearted look at various areas in London and comes from TNT's *London Guide*. This free magazine can be picked up from TNT's head office in Earls Court (14/15 Child's Place—it's 'hidden' at the end of the lane on the right). The times shown below are travel times from central London.

Acton W3 (30 minutes) Cheapish rent. Lots of antipodeans and Australasian pubs. Relatively noisy due to the busy A40 but conveniently close to the West End and safe enough to walk around.

Bayswater W2 (10 minutes) Sits on the edge of Hyde Park. Idyllic but expensive. You'd need lots of people per room to live here.

Brixton SW2 (15 minutes) Once dubbed a dangerous school

of squalor; now considered to be one of the grooviest places in town. Home to nightclubs The Fridge and Dogstar and Brockwell Park. Relatively cheap.

Camberwell SE5 (30 minutes) Cheap 'n' cheerful. Mix of students, squatters and crazy people. Home of the 'Camberwell Carrot'.

Camden NW1 (10 minutes) The bohemian centre for new age wannabees and home to the famous Camden Lock flea market. Trendy but expensive. Full of tourists on the weekends.

Chelsea SW3 (10 minutes) Prohibitively expensive. Flash cars and lots of rich people.

Chiswick W4 (20 minutes) Expensive. Good pubs. Don't pronounce the 'w'.

Clapham SW4 (20 minutes) Up and coming, the place for 'happening' twenty-somethings. A nice park (Clapham Common), British Rail connected and three tube stations. Great pubs, reasonable rent. Move in.

Ealing W5 (20 minutes) More expensive than Acton but has some OK pubs, restaurants and shops. Quaint, quiet and sleepy.

Earls Court SW5 (10 minutes) Cheap hostels but expensive to rent long-term pads. Close to High Street, Kensington and packed full of antipodeans most of whom have never met anyone British. Noisy, a bit grubby but a good home away from home for lonely travellers.

Fulham SW6 (10 minutes) A cheaper version of Chelsea and less pretentious. Quaint, classy and quiet without being dull.

Hackney E8 (25 minutes) Grotty and dirty with parts that are not so safe. Still, it's cheap.

Hammersmith W6 (15 minutes) Mid-price. Lots of concrete but close to the river. Good high street shopping, entertainment and a wide selection of restaurants.

Hampstead NW3 (15 minutes) One of the best areas in north London. Sip coffee in one of the relaxed, chilled and exceptionally cool coffee houses. Expensive.

Harlesden NW10 (20 minutes) Cheap. Big roundabout and plenty of traffic but cheap and central. A travellers' hubbub.

Hounslow TW3 (40 minutes) Next to Heathrow Airport.

Great place for plane-spotters.

Islington N1 (10 minutes) Rising in popularity and price. A great place to live and breath the pulse of London's centre. Good for those who can't afford to move to Camden.

Kensal Green W10 (20 minutes) A cultural vacuum. Not a decent pub in sight.

Kensington W8 (15 minutes) Expensive and posh.

Kentish Town NW5 (15 minutes) North London. Quite expensive but ideal for those who hanker after Camden which is down the road.

Kew TW9 (35 minutes) Quite expensive. Lovely gardens and ideal for botanists.

Kilburn NW6 (20 minutes) Cheap, cheerful and friendly. A lively antipodean foothold that won't break the bank.

Kings Cross N1 (5 minutes) Prices vary. Once famed as a bit of an underworld but improving with every year. Move in before the yuppies buy it up.

Kingston-upon-Thames KT1 & KT2 (30 minutes) Quite expensive. Richmondesque and pleasant in parts.

Maida Vale W9 (30 minutes) Fairly expensive and quiet with pretty canals.

New Cross SE14 (30 minutes) Cheap. Like Camberwell only less interesting.

Notting Hill W11 (10 minutes) Expensive. Home to Europe's biggest carnival in August. Rival to Camden for groovesville.

Peckham SE15 (30 minutes) See New Cross.

Richmond-upon-Thames TW9 & TW10 (30 minutes) Expensive. Very pleasant in summer with some lovely riverside pubs. Nice place to raise a family.

Shepherd's Bush W12 (15 minutes) Cheap rent, great transport, over-run with backpackers. A great outdoor flea market and thriving pub culture.

Stockwell SW9 (15 minutes) Cheapish. Brixton's (very) poor relation.

Willesden NW10 (20 minutes) Twinned with Harlesden although a bit more pleasant. Not much more.

Postcodes

Knowing how the postcodes in the UK work will help in your search for accommodation and work, especially in London where the postcode rather than the suburb is often mentioned in ads. The first half of the postcode indicates the suburban location while the second half indicates the location within the suburb.

While word processor spell checkers may hate UK postcodes, the system is very precise The letter shows geographical direction as follows: WC is West City, W is West London, SW is South West London, SE is South East London, E is East London, EC is East City, N is North London and NW is North West London.

The Gumboot

Peter Barr

An elderly gent entered the pub and asked, 'Got any beer, son?'.

I stared at him without answering for a moment and wondered if there was an English version of *Candid Camera*. I then spread my arms wide and replied, 'Yep, lots'.

He shot me a look as though I'd just told him John Major was my love child and croaked, 'No you fool, beer!'.

'Ah ... yes', I replied cautiously, beginning to doubt the octogenarian's mental stability, then swivelled on my heel and waved my arms like a game show host and announced, 'We have a lot of beer. This is a pub'.

'Listen you little bugger, what bloody beers have you got?', the gent spat, his creased face turning scarlet.

I paused, sensing his near-apoplectic state, and answered quietly, 'Er ... Castlemaine'.

Steam then shot from the poor man's ears like a neglected kettle and he lost balance and staggered uncontrollably around the pub. Patrons and bar stools were sent askew as he made his way erratically to the door, squawking like an injured cockatoo. I heard 'Bah!', 'Blast it all!', 'In all my born days!' and something about times being different when he was a lad, then the door slammed and he was gone forever.

My boss at The Gumboot was an Australian expat named Barry who thought it was a great laugh when I told him what had happened. Between guffaws, he told me that in England 'Beer isn't just beer, beer is beer'. After a moment my blank, vacant stare spurred him on, 'You see, there's beer and there's lager'. My expression remained static and he continued, 'To a beer person, lager's poison and to a lager person, beer tastes like shit!'.

I considered for a moment then asked if the twain ever met.

'A beer person will never drink lager,' he answered, 'and will harangue you mercilessly for hours on end for suggesting such a thing'.

'And lager people?', I enquired.

'They're not as discriminatory. A lager person will drink beer to impress a girl but won't enjoy it and, if you watch closely, you'll see they grimace slightly after each sip.'

I said I thought I understood, then asked if there was anything else I should know.

'One thing,' Barry replied, 'beer's brown and lager's yellow'.

OK, so they were different, that much was clear, although I still didn't understand what all the fuss was about. In Perth I'd ask for a beer, it'd come and I'd drink it. A very simple process. But in England, beer is important, as is everything about it, especially the drinking part. The Gumboot punters would expound the fascinating details of the inner workings of a brewery, and spout purple prose normally reserved for nineteenth century poetry on the subject of their favourite drop. Tetley's Bitter has great medicinal properties and virility-enhancing powers; no finer ale than Burtons will ever pass your lips; and Löwenbräu 'Strong' Lager gets you 'absolutely rat-arsed sharpish'. The exuberance of the clientele for their particular poison knew no bounds and the praise flowed like Skøl from the tap. But I winced every time I heard the smack of satisfied lips and the words, 'Ahh ... same again barman!'. I winced because I was privy to information I didn't want to know and secrets I struggled not to share. I knew the secrets of Barry's cellar.

Barry rarely worked behind the bar. His domain was the cellar. Everything down there was as he wanted—it was his nether world and he was Lord over it. I often thought of the cellar as Barry's own private little hell, for he made a good Lucifer.

I worked at The Gumboot for six months and, in retrospect, they were unfortunately the worst six months of my life. The work wasn't bad and generally the punters were fine. Barry was the problem. He gradually revealed himself to be an unstable, violent, angry alcoholic who took great pleasure in the misfortune of others. He denigrated his long-suffering girlfriend cruelly and often displayed unnerving misogynous tendencies, joking loudly about what he called 'men's sexual rights'. He would drink himself into a stupor then cause trouble and start fights in his own pub, becoming the staff's biggest concern on the busy weekends. He revelled in glory whenever he considered he'd drunk someone under the table, proclaiming the victory to all within earshot. He'd snigger to himself like a mischievous schoolboy when someone complimented him on the quality of his beer.

At the end of the night, he'd collect the 'slops' of the three different lagers into one bucket and scuttle down the creaking, ancient stairs to his hole in the ground. There, he would add the contents of the bucket to whichever lager we had sold the most of, then top it off with water. 'I'll have a good stock report this month, Pete', he'd confide conspiratorially, downing a pint of Tetley's Bitter.

I switched to Guinness and kept Barry's secrets of the cellar to myself, hated him for it and the countless other things he did to incense me so.

The Gumboot seemed like such a charming country pub when I first approached it. I had been given directions over the phone when I applied for the job of barman advertised in *TNT Magazine*. From London's Kings Cross station I took the Thameslink line for about 30 minutes to the town of St Kilda. Once there, 'Just ask anyone, everybody knows The Gumboot', the voice on the phone told me. And they did. I was directed to the centre of town where the pub sat in the shadow of the 30-foot-high, 400-year-old clock tower. I later learnt that Oliver Cromwell had once stopped for a pint in The Gumboot and that it was one of the oldest pubs in England. Furthermore, a punter once proudly informed me that St Kilda had more pubs than any other town in England. I feigned awe as I recalled that every town and village in the country seemed to make the same boastful claim.

There were however a lot of pubs in St Kilda; 'one on every corner' is a cliché but it's really not far from the truth in this town. I went to one called The Fighting Cocks which used to stage live cock-fights in a deep square pit in the centre of the pub. The pit's still there but thankfully the only feathers ruffled now are over football results and the latest sexual exploits of Tory party members.

Having found The Gumboot, I met the voice on the phone, Connie the landlady with whom I shared a pot of tea and a chat. She then introduced me to Barry who asked me what I drank and if I'd worked in a pub before. 'Yes, in Perth', I lied as he placed a pint of lager before me. We talked about Australia and the world and everything but the job, and by 10am I was employed and smashed. 'Right then,' Barry declared, 'That's that, let's go for a drink'. I don't remember much of the rest of that day, nor do I recall much of an interview taking place, but I woke up the following morning on the floor, in a room I didn't know, to the words, 'Here's 10 quid for the train. Go and get your stuff. You start tomorrow'.

I was being paid £110 per week for about 70 hours work. This included cleaning the pub as well as tending the bar. I supposed later that Barry knew exactly what he was doing during my 'interview'. I regarded it as a lesson in life. Food and board were included, apart from the £20 Connie took every month for meat and the tenner she required once a fortnight for vegies. Although I didn't actually have a bedroom or a bed for a month and a half while repairs were carried out, my space on the floor cost me nothing. I asked the builder working on the ceiling if it was a big job and he replied, 'Not really, she's just on the verge of collapse'. That night I snuggled up on the floorboards thinking of 'character and history' and how lucky I was to be there.

The customers were an interesting and eclectic bunch of people. On occasions, a few were drunkenly threatening but usually simply amusing. Veronica was suing a surgeon for malpractice but after half a dozen Bacardi and Cokes, was out of her wheelchair dancing like Tina Turner. Billjohn the Burglar—his own self-ascribed moniker—would ask me to look after packages wrapped in brown paper, give me a wink then go off 'on business'. When he returned, he'd ask if anybody had been looking for him. No-one ever was and he'd always say, 'Good, I'll have a pint then'. Jan and Terry began each night like newlyweds and by closing time were screaming for divorce. Like most comedy, it was simply life playing like a movie before me and it made me laugh.

Bob McCarthy wasn't a funny bloke. He and his four brothers entered the pub early one evening and it wasn't until they'd reached the bar and slurred their order that I realised how plastered they were. They were calm enough so I got their drinks, put them on the bar and said to Bob, 'That'll be six twenty-five thanks mate!'. He stared at me with an odd expression of silent indifference. In my professional manner—after all, I'd been at this for two months—I stated the amount again and gave him my best cool barman smile. Slowly he presented a £10 note, though his expression remained the same. I took the money to find Bob wasn't actually relinquishing it that easily and an absurd mini tug-of-war ensued. I would pull the tenner an inch my way then Bob would pull it the same distance his way, constantly staring, constantly silent. I was quickly fed up with the game, let go of the note and demanded he give me the money or leave the pub.

'You want me to pay for the drinks?', he replied with a tone of disbelief so strong you'd swear I'd demanded he leap from the clock tower. I said I didn't regard it as too unreasonable a request considering he was the punter and I was the barman. He then punched me in the face and I fell down. I got up thinking that something had gone drastically wrong in what was usually a fairly standard transaction. I was then pulled sideways by Kim the barmaid. Bob hurled his pint of lager at me and it exploded as it hit the wall, drenching Kim and myself with watery Castlemaine. Before the last droplets had settled on the floor, the boys were gone. I surveyed the carnage they'd left in their wake and felt a surge of pain flood my jaw.

Billjohn the Burglar came into the pub the next day and approached me wide-eyed, arms extended and palms upward. 'What the hell do you think you were doing you crazy Aussie?', he demanded. I guessed he was referring to the previous night's adventure as he continued, 'What are you doing taking on the McCarthy boys? You don't want to be upsetting the McCarthys, they're hard lads, well hard!'. For the next week and a half the town was abuzz with rumours that the crazy Aussie from The Gumboot had hassled the McCarthy family. I learnt that, according to St Kilda's legend, the McCarthy boys made the Kray brothers look like Bill and Ben the Flowerpot Men. It was decided that I must hold some bizarre death wish: people avoided me in droves, the pub had never been quieter and Barry more annoyed. 'Where's all the bloody punters?', he would wail. It was great.

Billjohn the Burglar said he'd stand by me and stole toasted baked bean sandwiches for my lunch. A symbol of his loyalty, I guess. I tried to tell him that the pub had a kitchen but it seemed to make him happy that he could help out a fellow rebel in such a way. I discovered a couple of days later that the sandwiches were given out to the homeless by The Salvation Army. I never saw Bob McCarthy again. I figured he realised you just don't mess with a crazy Aussie barman who eats stolen food and sleeps on the floor.

After a while, I left St Kilda. I left the pub and the folk who drank there and I left Barry with his foolish secrets. Later I realised what a terrible time I'd had at The Gumboot, especially compared to the bar work experiences of others, and it made me angry. At times it still bothers me, but somehow it all seems worthwhile and I'm glad I worked there. Life's full of different experiences.

Settling in

Bryan Havenhand

This chapter covers a range of issues that you're likely to come across not too long after arriving in the UK.

Obtaining a national insurance number

You will normally be required to obtain a National Insurance number and provide this to your employer. If you are only working in casual and odd jobs this may not be such an issue. Your employer should have an application form for you to fill in if your agency hasn't supplied one already. Otherwise you can organise it by visiting a local Department of Social Services (DSS) office. You can find the local office by telephoning the main London DSS office on (0171) 301 8000. Money collected under the National Insurance scheme goes towards the various categories of benefits including unemployment payments, the health scheme and state pensions. You may be eligible for a rebate of monies paid under the National Insurance scheme. An organisation that may be able to assist with this is Global Select at 70 North End Road, West Kensington, London W14 OSJ. Tel: (0171) 371 1616.

Opening a bank account

Banks in the UK have a peculiar reputation: it is hard to open an account with them. See Jeannie Zakharov's chapter for an account of her troubles. Certainly there is a fair amount of paper work involved and the UK banks are less than keen on having you as a customer knowing that you will most likely be a temporary customer who won't be handing them sizeable amounts of cash on a regular basis. (Many social security payments are paid through the post offices.) If you try to open an account before you have a job your chances of success are slim.

If you opt to open an account after you arrive in the UK there are plenty of banks to choose from. There are four main 'high street' banks: Barclays, Lloyds (American Express travellers cheques are cashed commission free), Midland (Thomas Cook travellers cheques are cashed commission free) and NatWest. In addition there are smaller banks such as TSB and the Royal Bank of Scotland along with large building societies and building societies that have become banks such as Abbey National and Halifax Building Society. Some antipodeans have found the smaller banks and the building societies friendlier to deal with.

To open an account you'll need two references, one of which should be a reference from your bank at home, identification, an address and preferably a job. You'll want to open a current account which will come with a cheque book and a cheque or debit card. It is not uncommon to see customers write cheques at supermarket cash registers but to do this you need the cheque card as proof of your signature. You can also use this card to withdraw funds from ATMs. You may wish to discuss the linking of your credit card with your current account to provide more flexibility.

In the same way that the Commonwealth and Westpac banks in Australia allow customers to use the ATMs of both banks (albeit at an additional charge) so there are similar arrangements in the UK. While you'll be able to get more information on this once you have chosen a bank, the banking groups are as follows: Midland, NatWest, Royal Bank of Scotland, TSB, Clydesdale and Northern; and Barclays, Lloyds, Royal Bank of Scotland and Bank of Scotland. There is also a Link arrangement of ATMs which joins the TSB and Cooperative banks and most major building societies. Knowing which ATMs you can use will allow you easier access to your money. You'll also find that your bank will provide some level of telephone banking including the payment of bills, so you may be interested in following up on this.

Depending on your plans, it is best to find an employment agency that you will be happy to work for and have them assist you in opening an account. Most agencies will have an arrangement with a bank which will let you do this. Most likely it will be their bank which will ensure that your pay cheques can be credited directly to your account. Once you have a bank account into which your pay is automatically credited you probably won't have to visit your bank branch very often at all. This will save you shoe leather and time.

Food shopping

You'll find food, especially fresh food, more expensive than at home, but that doesn't mean you have to subsist on baked beans and toast. To give you some idea a Big Mac costs about £1.85; use the current exchange rate to get an idea of the difference.

If you have the time and enjoy shopping with a difference try the street markets, these are scattered throughout London and each is distinguishable from the other by the type of food for sale and the price.

The Church Street (NW8 and W2) market is open Tuesday to Saturday and is the biggest general market in central London. The Brixton market (SW9) is open from Monday to Saturday and has a wide variety of African and Caribbean food along with fish and all the usual vegetables and fruit. If you end up living in inner London you're bound to find a market not too far away. The best time to shop on price is Saturday afternoons when prices are cut to get rid of what is left.

If markets are not your thing then there are plenty of supermarkets that are price competitive and predictable. The four major supermarket chains in the UK are Tesco (the largest), J Sainsbury, Asda and Safeway, with nearly half of all food sales between them. The following list is a sample of prices collected in early 1999 from a medium sized Tesco supermarket:

potatoes £1 per kg
carrots £1.20 per kg
tomatoes £1.50 per kg
pure orange juice £2 for 2 litres
pork sausages 30p for 100 grams
white rice £1 per kg

brown rice £1.50 per kg
Basmati rice £2.30 per kg
chicken about £3 for 1.5 kg
Kellogs corn flakes 90p for 250 grams
milk 90p for 4 pints (2.27 litres).

Health

Australians and New Zealanders are covered for basic and emergency healthcare and subsidised dental care through the National Health Service (NHS) courtesy of a reciprocal agreement between these countries. The agreement does not cover pre-existing medical conditions. There is no particular registration process but when you visit a doctor you need to take your passport (Australians should also have their Medicare card) and advise medical staff at the time of treatment that you wish to be treated under the Reciprocal Health Care Agreement with Australia or New Zealand. While the best option is to have the treatment bulk billed to the NHS, doctors are not obliged to bulk bill so you may need to pay for a consultation and then claim back your due. Otherwise, find a doctor who will bulk bill by asking around. You're also able to visit an outpatients' department of a public hospital and you have access to a public ward in an NHS hospital for emergency treatment. Apart from an absolute emergency the chances of getting to see an NHS dentist are minuscule. All the more reason to visit a dentist at home before you leave.

Homesickness

Sometimes you may find yourself with the homesick blues, but there are plenty of cures including adjourning to your favourite Australasian pub or ringing home (although this may make things worse). Keep an eye on the Australasian press, especially *TNT Magazine*, for social events for those from down-under. Australians could visit Australia House at The Strand, London WC2 (the nearest Underground stations are Aldwych and Temple) to read the newspapers or talk to others with a familiar accent while New Zealanders can drop into New Zealand House, 80 Haymarket SW1 (the nearest Underground station is Piccadilly Circus) for a similar pickup. The high commissions are also located at these addresses and you'll go there for matters relating to passports and other things like voting absentee in elections.

If you want to get your hands on some Australian or New Zealand products visit the Australia Shop at 26 Henrietta Street, London, Tel: (0171) 836 2292, or the New Zealand Shop at 7 Royal Arcade, London SW1Y 4UY, Tel: (0171) 930 4587, just behind New Zealand House. At the Australia Shop you can buy Australian products like Driza-Bone (now owned by the Brits), Akubra hats, food including vegemite, and confectionery, maps, travel guides, souvenirs and videos. The New Zealand Shop has a similar range of home-grown merchandise including All Black training jerseys. Perfect if you are stuck for presents to give to the locals ('I had it air freighted especially').

One thing you'll notice about the UK media is that, short of a natural disaster, a thumping cricket win or an outstanding performance in rugby union, Australia and New Zealand for all intents and purposes don't exist. Of course they do exist, and this news gap is filled in part by the Australasian press in London. More recently the ABC's website, www.abc.net.au, provides a fantastic connection to home for Australians. You can even listen to local radio over the Internet in real time! New Zealanders can keep up with home news through TV NZ's website at www.tvnz.nz. You may also wish to subscribe to *NZ Newsgram*, a monthly newsletter at NZ$2.50 per issue plus postage. Contact *NZ Newsgram* by telephone on (09) 274 1917 or email nzibs@ix.co.nz.

Internet cafes

Once you've settled in you might want to make regular use of an Internet cafe for sending emails home or just surfin' the net. *TNT Magazine* publishes a current list each week and also publishes the list on the TNT website www.tntmag.co.uk. Compare the price of accessing the Internet through these cafes as there can be some significant differences, especially in minimum charges, but expect to pay around £6 per hour or £1.50 per 10 minutes. Membership of BUNAC will provide a discount of 30% at one Internet centre.

Entertainment

London is a feast of entertainment, from the local busker to world famous concert entertainers. Even if you are constrained by money there are many standby, late entry and half price arrangements, so there is little that a streetwise operator is excluded from. You'll pick up the contacts and hints with time. Apart from your growing circle of friends and acquaintances—who may or may not have the same tastes as you—the best quick reference of what's happening is *Time Out*, available weekly from newsagents everywhere for £1.80. Start with Time Out's *London Visitors' Guide* for £4 from newsagents for a quick view of the action in London.

Post offices

Post offices are open from 9am to 5.30pm during the week, and from 9am to midday on Saturday morning. Within the UK mail can be sent first or second class with first class meaning overnight delivery. Mail can be sent to you c/- Poste Restante, Trafalgar Square Post Office, 24-28 William IV Street, London WC2N. This post office is open from 8am to 8pm Monday to Friday and 9am to 8pm on Saturdays. Mail will be held for four weeks and you'll require a passport or some other identification when picking up mail. The nearest Underground station is Charing Cross.

Taxis

There are two types of taxis in London, the black cab and the minicab, but black cabs aren't all black and minicabs aren't all small.

Drivers of the black cabs are in a class of their own, they don't see their work as a job but as a calling. In order to qualify for a licence to drive a black cab they must gain 'the knowledge' required to never get lost (well almost never). These cabs are metered and they can be quite expensive with prices starting at around £5 for a five minute ride, so it's best to have three or four people to make the cost reasonable. In addition a 10% tip is expected, though a rounding up of the fare is usually adequate. Black cabs can be hailed from the footpath when the yellow sign on the roof is on.

Minicabs can be any sort of car with a two-way radio that is connected to a base station. These cabs had a bad reputation but legislation in 1998 forced the operators to clean up their act. The plus is that these cabs are much cheaper than the black cabs. Minicabs must be booked by phone and are not metered so you should settle on a fare before beginning the journey. When you settle into an area, find out which minicab operator covers your area and keep their phone number on you. They are handy late at night when public transport winds down. There is one minicab company, Lady Cabs, which has women drivers and its cars are available only to women. The minicab driver's knowledge of London is not as good as the drivers of the black cabs so you may have to assist with directions.

Telephones

British Telecom, previously publicly owned but now privatised, competes across a range of services with Mercury. Both companies operate public phone boxes that look nothing like Dr Who's Tardus. It is worth picking up a telephone card from a newsagent or post office as most public phone boxes will accept them along with cash. You need to remember that local calls are timed. The phone boxes in central London are decorated with calling cards offering to satisfy just about every sexual fantasy possible for both men (mostly) and women.

London is divided into an 0171 area which is central London and an 0181 area which is outer London. From 22 April 2000 there will be some significant changes to London and other phone numbers. The 0171 and 0181 numbers will be replaced by 020 and the '7' or '8' will be added to the front of the existing seven digit number to make phone numbers with eight digits. For example, (0171) 443 2234 becomes (020) 7443 2234. There will also be changes to telephone numbers in Cardiff, Coventry, Portsmouth, Southampton and Northern Ireland at the same time. The rest of the country remains unchanged.

As previously suggested having your own mobile phone that operates in the UK is an option, albeit a more expensive one. A mobile phone can be very handy when it comes to having agencies and possible employers contact you. However, apart from cost you should look seriously at the issue of security in case of theft, at the very least your phone should require a PIN to be entered before it operates.

If you wish to switch to a local supplier there are many phone companies chasing business in London and you'll have no shortage of choice with very good prices on offer. You'll find plenty of advertising in the Australasian press. These companies include Alpha Telecom (Tel: 0800 279 3156), Communications 2000 (Tel: 0800 634 2000), First Telecom (Tel: 0800 458 4646 or www.first-telecom.com), Primus (Tel: 0800 036 0020 or www.primustel.com), RSLCOM (Tel: 0800 074 0404), Speedial (Tel: 0800 376 7676) and ValuCall (Tel: 0800 496 5000) along with the big players like British Telecom. Prices start from around 10p per minute to Australia and 12p per minute to New Zealand, but these rates usually require a minimum starting account of about £30.

Tipping

Tipping is becoming common, especially in London. It is normal to provide a tip at restaurants of about 10-15% when there is no service charge. Hairdressers and black cab drivers are also usually provided with a tip but rounding up is acceptable. Of course if the cost is £2.90, you'll be expected to do a little more than round up to £3.

Transport

It should be pointed out that London Transport (the authority responsible for public transport in London) levies a fine of at least £10 for fare evasion which can hurt, especially if you are on a tight budget. London Transport must also be experimenting with the Chinese technique of 'public vilification'. I saw a large poster at Kings Cross station that listed the names of those who had been caught for fare evasion. It is highly unlikely in a city the size of London that this would be much of a deterrent but the fine could be.

There are some transport discounts which you should avail yourselves of if eligible. The Young Persons Railcard is for those between 16 and 25 years. The card is worth obtaining as you'll get about one-third off most rail fares in addition to other discounts. Pick up an application form from railway station offices or contact an authorised student travel office for full details. National Express is the national bus line and it travels to 1200 destinations around the UK. It has a discount card which costs £8 per year for those between 16 and 25 years of age. This card provides discounts of up to 30%. When in the UK ring 0990 010 104 to find out the location of your nearest National Express agent so you can organise a card. For more details visit the National Express website at www.nationalexpress.co.uk.

VAT

You'll come across this sooner or later. It stands for 'value-added tax' and is similar to the GST which New Zealanders are used to and Australians are about to become accustomed to. VAT was introduced in the UK on April Fool's Day in 1973 at the rate of 10%, though it is now 17.5%. There are a considerable number of exempt and zero-rated goods including books, magazines, rent and footwear. If you visit the UK for less than 365 days you are normally able to claim the tax back through the VAT Refund Scheme. To do this you need to obtain VAT receipt vouchers from the retailer but different retailers will require different levels of minimum spending, usually from about £40, for you to obtain a VAT receipt voucher. You are then able to use these vouchers at the airport on your way out of the UK to claim your refund.

Studying

If you have a particular interest then there are plenty of short courses available in the UK. Check out *Oncourse, Floodlight* and *Summer Floodlight*, all available from newsagents and some bookshops for between £2 and £4. For adult education courses across the UK contact NIACE (National Institute of Adult Continuing Education) at 21 De Montfort Street, Leicester LE1 7GE. Tel: (0116) 204 4200. Website: www.niace.org.uk. It's one way to meet locals who have similar interests to your own. A means of accessing information on academic study in the UK is to approach the British Council at home. In Australia you'll find the British Council at PO Box 88, Edgecliff NSW 2027. Tel: (02) 9326 2022. Fax: (02) 9327 4868. Email: bcsydney@bc-sydney.sprint.com. In New Zealand the Council is at PO Box 1812, Wellington 1. Tel: (04) 472 6049. Fax: (04) 473 6261. Email: info@bc-wellington.sprint.com. Studying for certification in the UK is expensive though there are a number of scholarships for those suitably qualified.

Measurements

Surprisingly, many measurements are still expressed in imperial units including miles, pints and pounds. So if you have grown up with metric, check the conversion table at the end of this book. This adherence to an old system is symbolic of why the Brits are having such a hard time grappling with the concept of the UK being part of Europe. Antipodeans can probably understand this difficulty.

Activity camps

Heather Farish

Abseiling, canoeing, fencing, horseriding, archery and windsurfing are just some of the activities you can be involved in when working in a children's activity camp in Britain. The summer camps of America receive a lot of publicity and large numbers of Australians spend a summer or two working there. However, how many of these people know about or consider working in a camp in Britain?

I was fortunate to have the opportunity to spend two months working in a children's activity camp in Britain during a recent summer. As is the case for most of these camps, they are located in very scenic parts of the country. My camp, Llwyn Filly, is located on the border between England and Wales near Hay-on-Wye. Being an old farmhouse renovated to accommodate camps, it is full of atmosphere. It is close to the Brecon Beacons National Park, the Wye Valley and lakes.

Llwyn Filly is a small camp with a staff of 10 catering for groups of about 40. The staff consists of group leaders, kitchen staff, activity instructors and a manager to keep an eye on everything. During the school term school groups with children between the ages of eight and 12 attend the camp. In the holidays individuals involved in pony trekking attend. A normal day for the children has them up at about 7.30am for breakfast and leaving for morning activities at about 8.30am. If they are away for the day they take a cut lunch and return about 5.15pm. At 6.00pm they have dinner, with evening entertainment from 7.00pm to 9.00pm. It's then a drink of hot chocolate and off to bed.

I worked as a kitchen assistant so I prepared and served meals and cleaned up afterwards. This routine allowed about four hours off during the day. All staff members had one day off each week and most used it for a well-earned break away from camp.

I explored the nearby town of Hay-on-Wye several times. It is easy to spend time there as it has dozens of book shops. In some circles it is known as the 'Book Capital' of the world. I went to Hereford and to Brecon, both of which are only about 50km away. I spent time walking across the fields, over the stiles and along roads between tall hedges. I also spent time exploring that great British institution, the pub. There are many in the surrounding area and they are a very pleasant place to sample the local beers and ciders.

There are other positions available in activity camps for drivers, cooks, couriers, TEFL (teaching English as a foreign language) teachers, nurses, group leaders, administration assistants and instructors. The instructors may be involved in a number of activities or just one, depending on the size of the camp. Sailing, canoeing, windsurfing, pony trekking, archery, fencing, judo, abseiling, shooting, motor sports, orienteering and caving are among the more popular activities. The instructors spend the morning and afternoon instructing children in addition to doing regular spells of night duty.

Often in the evenings after finishing the kitchen I had the opportunity to participate in the entertainment. This could include bonfires, sports tournaments, amateur dramatics, 'Cluedo', hieroglyphics and 'Dangle in the Dingle'. Two or three times a week I was on night duty. This involves giving the children a drink of hot chocolate, getting them into bed and supervising until they are asleep. At times this is a very trying exercise especially if the children are homesick, ill or just not wanting to go to sleep. As a result, those on night duty often don't get to bed until well after midnight.

Facilities for staff are somewhat basic but quite livable. My accommodation was provided, but it was a tent in the orchard next to the house. I had a mattress on the ground, the luckier ones had their mattresses on top of bread crates with a doona. There is a staff bathroom and a staff room with a television and video. The staff room is usually used as a retreat from the children when it all becomes too hectic.

I participated in two of the activities, abseiling and pony trekking, neither of which I had done before. Although my stomach was full of butterflies when I backed out over the precipice for my first abseiling descent, I tried to reassure the watching children by keeping a brave face. The descent down the 20 metre wall was strange and scary but I was elated upon reaching the bottom in one piece.

Lucky for me, who had only ever been on a horse once, the horses we rode were quite docile. The trails used for horseriding meander through spectacular countryside. We rode along tracks in the Brecon Beacons, looking down on Lake Llanghorse and the surrounding countryside. The yellows, greens and browns of the fields, the hedges, roads and farmhouses resemble a carefully woven patchwork quilt.

The Llwyn Filly centre is just one of 19 in Britain run by PGL Adventure. These are found from Dalguise, Scotland in the north to Devon in south west England. There is also a centre on the island of Guernsey and another ten in France and Spain. It is possible to begin working in Britain and then transfer across the channel.

PGL Adventure camps cater for children of all ages, family groups and for instructing groups of teachers. The staff are predominantly British although there are a number of Australians and New Zealanders. The centres open for varying periods between February and December and you can work for the whole season or part of it. The pay varies depending on your work and responsibilities. I earned about £40 a week on top of meals and accommodation. Camp work is not something you do if you want to make money. You are encouraged to undertake training and to complete qualifications in areas such as first aid, canoeing, food hygiene and life saving.

The work gives you the opportunity to meet and work with the locals, learn about the British way of life and to spend time in one area rather than just travelling through. The camp experience is one of the highlights of my travels.

A lowdown on work

Bryan Havenhand

Armed with your work visa, a bit of knowledge and the right attitude you won't be without a job in London for long. Other parts of the UK may be a bit slower though cities such as Edinburgh, Manchester and Birmingham do provide a range of opportunities. Edinburgh, for example, is a financial centre with many banking and insurance firms providing temporary positions for people with experience in these fields.

Jobs are available because the economy is doing very nicely (the unemployment rate is about 5%, though this does vary significantly in different parts of the country) and because many London firms rely heavily on temps. Employing temps rather than employing permanent staff allows a firm to keep its costs lower. Australians and New Zealanders have a reputation in the UK as good workers (this may surprise many) so they are sought after by many employers. Manpower, a temporary employment agency, estimates that between 7 and 8% of the workforce is now employed on a temporary basis. While this is not a pleasant statistic for locals wanting secure employment, it is fine for those wanting some short-term employment while travelling.

While temps do not receive some of the benefits of permanent employment such as holidays and sick leave (though there are exceptions), on the other hand they receive a higher hourly rate and have flexibility of employment which allows them to travel between placements. Over the last 24 months the recruitment industry in the UK (in reality, mostly in London) has had considerable growth and temporary placements (as opposed to permanent placements) accounted for over 90% of the sector's activity. Secretarial and clerical positions accounted for 29% of all temporary work while blue collar positions accounted for 26%. The other 45% was split into smaller occupational groupings. In an average year the 63,000 employment consultants in the UK find temporary jobs for 900,000 people. This is reassuring to those from the antipodes who think it will be hard to get work in the UK.

Taxation

If you are working through an agency they should assist you with taxation matters. However if not, or if you are organising your own work, you will be required to fill out a P46 form at the start of each job so that this can be sent to the tax office (called Inland Revenue) where the level of tax you are required to pay is assessed. Until this is finalised you may find yourself being taxed at a flat 25% on all earnings. At the end of each tax year (which ends on 5 April) you will receive a summary of all wages and tax paid for the financial year just past. If you only worked part of the financial year you may be due a partial refund on tax paid. You can lodge a tax rebate claims form with Inland Revenue to get this, however, if you are leaving the country you should place this in the hands of a tax agent who will send you a refund for which there will be a small charge. You'll find addresses for these companies in London's Australasian press but one such company run by Australafrikiwis (a variation on antipodeans) is 1st Contact, Piccadilly House, 33 Regent Street, London SW1Y 4ZT. Tel: (0171) 577 3636. Tax rates change but at present the following PAYE rates apply: the first £4195 is tax free, the next £4300 is taxed at 20%, the next £22,800 is taxed at 23%, and the remainder is taxed at 40%.

Limited liability companies

For those working short-term contracts the option of setting up a limited company is appealing. It means you receive payment for your services without any tax or National Insurance deductions. This is possible because your company will bill the company or agency you are working for and it will pay your company. However, it means that you are responsible for ensuring that taxation and National Insurance obligations are met.

The advantages of working through a limited liability company are that it improves your cash flow, and it allows you to earn more because you can claim for expenses that are allowable for your occupation. The disadvantages are that it involves some degree of paperwork including setting up the company, maintaining records, fulfilling legal obligations and filing end of year accounts. If you have the potential to earn substantial amounts, over about £50,000, you will have to register for VAT as well. A danger of having money to spend before you pay tax is that you spend too much, so you will need to budget your expenditure.

There are several businesses in London that specialise in setting up and maintaining companies for contractors including Australians and New Zealanders. There will be a charge for this service, including the purchase of the company, which will be about £100, but it will relieve you of the paperwork. One such company is 1st Contact, Piccadilly House, 33 Regent Street, London SW1Y 4ZT. Tel: (0171) 577 3636. Others are advertised in the Australasian press and you'll probably come across personal recommendations. First work out your earning capacity before committing yourself to a company, as the process may not be worth it. 1st Contact recommends those earning more than £4 per hour can benefit from a limited company. Do not view a limited company as a way to avoid paying tax. Inland Revenue has long arms and can catch up with you in Australia or New Zealand.

Occupational groups

While the working holiday visa does not allow you—with some exceptions—to work in a job that furthers your career, this aspect of the visa is a grey area. While it may mean that immigration officers expect you to only work serving beers, this is not the reality. Strictly speaking it may mean a qualified accountant working as an assistant accountant. However, even an experience such as this can add shine to a CV back home. You may wish to talk this issue through with the agency you sign up with to see how the rules will impact on you. If you have a visa based on ancestry or a British or another EU country passport then this problem will not apply. The remainder of this chapter provides a general idea of available positions, requirements and rates of pay in the UK.

Accounting, banking and finance

London is one of the key financial centres of the world so it is not surprising that those with good qualifications and some experience are in a good position to command good salaries. There is plenty of temporary work for accountants, even those who have recently qualified, though those with at least two years experience can command better positions and higher salaries. There is also a shortage of those with specialist skills such as auditing and financial controllers.

Having good quality computer skills across a range of programs will make you more employable. Getting some additional computer skills and gaining broader experience before going to London may be a good option as it will result in you getting better paying jobs more quickly. An accounts clerk can figure on earning about £8-10 per hour while a qualified accountant can earn about £20-30 per hour. A systems specialist can earn about £15-50 per hour. However, because many temporary accountants are working on project-orientated contracts, long hours will normally be involved to make a deadline. Accountants are equally likely to find themselves working in private or public organisations or in private practice. In London demand for accountants heats up towards the end of the calendar year and can continue through to the end of February.

The City of London survives on its banking and finance sector and this sector relies heavily on temps for a wide range of jobs. Positions requiring specific knowledge and experience include traders, dealers and analysts in a range of areas including international equities, futures and options, bonds and swaps. You should have excellent broad-based computer skills but especially Visual Basic, Excel and Access. You should get about £12 per hour in your first position but this can rise to the mid-twenties after some experience.

The best way to find a position is through agencies and many specialise in the financial area. When you make contact with an agency in London they will want to see your qualifications, at least two references (preferably from previous employers), your CV with details of your accounting and computer skills, and your passport.

Agriculture

There is a wide range of positions available in agriculture from fully qualified and experienced agriculturists to casual labourers required at harvest time, though there can be a lot of competition here from European students. The great benefit of working on farms is that you see another side of British life not experienced by many travellers. (You can also discover farm life through WWOOF, see chapter 17). Most farm positions will include accommodation and food. Pay for farm relief work will vary from £100-200 per week. However, relief work will require applicants to have at least three years experience with appropriate animals or crops. Wages from harvest work will depend on the amount picked and this will vary from crop to crop and depends on your speed.

While some occupational groups are specifically banned from practising in the UK while on a working holiday visa, the veterinary profession is not one of these groups. Vets are allowed to seek work through an agency and there are agencies through which qualified and experienced vets can obtain placements throughout the UK. Wendy Alexander, the copy editor of this book, worked as a locum vet in the UK while on a working holiday visa. Using an agency she was placed in various veterinary practices around the country allowing practice owners to take a holiday. She was provided with a flat and car (often including petrol) at each practice, in addition to a salary of around £100 per day.

It is a legal requirement and therefore essential that vets register and are admitted to membership of the Royal College of Veterinary Surgeons (RCVS) before engaging in any type of veterinary work in the UK. Details of the RCVS membership application process—which includes forwarding a letter or certificate of good professional standing from your current registration authority—are available at the RCVS website: www.rcvs.org.uk. Alternatively, contact the RCVS at Belgravia House, 62-64 Horseferry Road, London SW1P 2AF. Tel: (0171) 222 2001. Fax: (0171) 222 2004. E-mail: admin@rcvs.org.uk. The current membership fee is £170 per annum. As part of the registration process involves attending in person one of the fortnightly registration meetings to complete the formalities, don'texpect to be registered within a day of arriving in the UK.

Domestic positions

These include nannies, mothers' helps (housekeepers/ nannies) and carers. Despite the publicity surrounding the deaths of two children in the care of nannies (an English nanny in America and an Australian nanny in the UK), there is no shortage of demand for appropriately qualified and experienced nannies. Families where both parents work is very common, and with young children, the only solution is to employ a nanny. Often the families are at the higher end of the income scale so nannies may find themselves in very pleasant suburbs. Both live-in and live-out positions are available with live-in positions starting at around £150 per week with board and food usually an additional part of the arrangement. Live-in nannies will also be expected to undertake household duties, which usually means a fairly long day. However, there are some perks such as going on family holidays, even if it means some childcare as well. It is highly unlikely that men will be able to find a position in this area unless it is in a family with boys who are sports mad and where the parents are liberal minded.

Other positions available in the home include mothers' helps, which usually means assisting mothers with young children, and again this can be a live-in or daily position. There can be many variations of this type of work and pay will vary accordingly.

Carers are people who look after elderly men and women in their own homes. This can be a live-in or daily position but with live-in positions you may need to be available day and night. Duties will often include cooking, bathing and dressing, taking the client shopping, general household duties and grocery shopping. Some positions involve looking after physically or mentally disabled people. Pay rates vary, but for a live-in position you can think in terms of a starting figure of about £200 per week plus your board and food. People looking for these positions often need a considerable degree of patience. Many elderly people are rather fixed in what food they like to eat and how things should be done and may have limited or slow mobility.

While many of these domestic positions are advertised in the press it is often best to go through an agency so you have some backup in difficult times. Agencies know the pay rates and conditions of employment and will be able to find another position for you if you do not get on with the family or person you are working with. In all cases qualifications are useful, along with a couple of references. These positions can also be found in areas outside of the major cities. It is important to have a flexible attitude and enjoy working with people.

Education and teaching

Although there are some positions in educational administration and some university and college jobs, along with teaching English as a foreign language (TEFL), by far the bulk of education positions are for primary and secondary teachers, mostly in state schools. The greatest demand is for primary teachers. Demand also exists for some disciplines in secondary schools including maths, science, modern European languages, music, craft, design and technology, and home economics, though this list changes over time. There are far fewer positions for humanities teachers. The British teaching year is only 195 days so the working holiday visa allows holders to work as supply (casual or emergency) teachers without contravening the rules of the working holiday visa.

TEFL teaching is a good prospect for those with the appropriate qualifications. There are over 300 English-teaching schools in the UK that have TEFL courses but not all of these schools have year-round programs. The busiest period for these schools is over summer when many students, from Europe in particular, come to the UK to study in intensive courses. Schools are mostly found in London, Oxford, Cambridge, Canterbury, Brighton, Hastings, Eastbourne and Bournemouth with some in other areas. You'll need a TEFL certificate or equivalent, preferably some experience and for the UK, you'll need to have a fairly neutral accent—a broad Australian strine or New Zealand twang won't do. Teachers can be taken on for a whole summer course, which will usually include classroom activities and recreational activities, or on an hourly basis for classroom teaching only. For a whole course contract, pay may begin at £100 per week up to double that amount. Sometimes you'll get accommodation and food as well, though in the case of residential courses this may mean you take turns at being on duty at night. For information on TEFL teaching, refer to the book *Teaching Overseas* which is listed in the appendix.

The most common form of employment in primary and secondary schools is as a supply teacher. This involves you filling a vacancy for a day, a week or several months. It is not surprising that the most readily available positions are in what might be called challenging schools, especially in London. Many of these schools have an amazing mix of ethnic groups and experience in this type of school will assist you with finding work, not that there is any shortage of work for general supply teachers. The start of the new school year up until Christmas often sees a heavy demand for supply teachers with positions lasting from a couple of days to several weeks.

On average, supply teachers can expect to earn about £85 to £95 per day. Sometimes there will be higher rates for longer term placements. Teachers usually work from 8.30am to 3.30pm. There are three terms beginning with the autumn term from early September to Christmas, the spring term from early January to about mid-April, and the summer term from early May to the end of July. The exact start and finish dates can vary a bit between boroughs (local councils) as much management of schools is the responsibility of the boroughs. There is growing talk about implementing a five-term system of eight weeks each term, but this could take ages to eventuate.

There are also supply teaching positions in areas outside London and some agencies, such as Quality Teachers, are readily able to offer positions in cities such as Manchester and Birmingham or in south eastern England. There is a much smaller chance of teaching in Scotland or Northern Ireland as a longer term commitment is usually required, which is not always possible with a working holiday visa. However, while it is difficult to find an agency that can offer supply teaching positions in Scotland, an enterprising Australian who found a teaching position in Scotland has put together a kit to explain how to do this (see chapter 15).

Australian and New Zealand teaching qualifications are not automatically recognised by UK teaching authorities. Antipodean teachers are initially ineligible for Qualified Teacher Status (QTS) which is required to teach in state schools. Instead, Australians and New Zealanders need to first work as a 'licensed teacher' until a period of teaching has been completed successfully, which sometimes involves additional training, before QTS is granted. There is some variation in the QTS requirements depending on the employer (the borough education authority or the school board). In practice, depending on the QTS process does not greatly affect the ability of Australians to teach or the level of pay received. In order to gain employment as a teacher you require:

- a valid work visa
- teaching qualifications along with a certified transcript
- an official letter from the state police department giving police clearance (this is a requirement for anyone working with children)
- names and addresses of three recent employment referees
- some spare passport photos
- details of teaching experience.

There are four ways to find a teaching position:

- go through a teacher recruitment agency
- apply directly to schools (in the case of private schools)

- apply to a borough education authority or
- apply to an advertisement in publications such as *The Times Educational Supplement* or *The Guardian.*

However, unless you are eligible to apply for a long-term position and have a good knowledge of the national curriculum, the last three options are not viable (unless the borough runs an agency). For those on a working holiday visa, agencies are the ideal option and there are several in Australia and New Zealand. They can show you around the national curriculum, explain how the education system works in general, as well as provide support and allow you to work continuously by placing you in another school when an existing supply position comes to a finish. Some provide teaching materials and photocopiers for use and assist you in settling into London.

There are many recruitment agencies in the UK, mostly in London. If you wish to organise your teaching after arriving in London check the *TNT Magazine* for a list of agencies. Many boroughs are active in recruiting supply teachers and this is sometimes a reflection of the difficulties encountered by teachers in these local schools. For a full list of borough education authorities to which you may apply contact The British Council, Education Information Service, PO Box 88, Edgecliff NSW 2027. Tel: (02) 9326 2365. Fax: (02) 9327 4868 or PO Box 1812, Wellington. Tel: (04) 472 6049. Fax: (04) 473 6261. This is a reasonable option after you have become familiar with the UK school system and know where you will be living. Always try to minimise your travelling time. However, for the first time, it is hard to beat the services provided by the teacher recruitment agencies. In all the above cases, you will need a face-to-face interview before placement, in addition to gaining some understanding of the national curriculum.

Engineering and construction

While engineering doesn't have the public profile of say teaching or IT, there is plenty of work in the engineering field for those with appropriate qualifications and experience. Like teaching and IT, it is best to find work through agencies and some specialise in the engineering and construction area. There is plenty of work both in London and throughout the UK, which allows you to experience different parts of the country. Work can be found with local authorities, British engineering firms or large international contractors, sometimes leading to placements in other parts of the world. Work across all engineering disciplines can be found along with architectural work, estimating, draughting and managerial responsibilities. Pay will vary significantly depending on the position and location but will readily match pay down-under.

Healthcare

There is a healthy demand for health professionals both in the National Health Service (NHS) and in private practice. The working holiday visa allows those in the following occupations to continue in their career: nurses (via an agency), occupational therapists, physiotherapists, radiographers, and speech and language therapists.

Dentists

Dentists are not permitted to work using the working holiday visa so they must be using another permit or have employer sponsorship. For details regarding registration in the UK you should contact the Dental Council at 37 Wimpole Street, London W1M 8DQ. Tel: (0171) 486 2171. This is necessary because you will need to have your usual doctor fill out part of the registration form regarding your health. Upon arrival in the UK you'll need to visit the Dental Council in person with all the necessary forms to finalise registration. Work is available in private practices and as a locum with payment at around £20 per hour.

Dental nurses

Dental nurses don't need to be qualified to work in the UK but they do need to pass an examination or to have worked at an equivalent level in their home country. It is best to make use of an agency that specialises in this area and once in the system you can expect to earn about £6-7 per hour. Dental nurses need to be registered with the Association of British Surgery Assistants, 110 London Street, Fleetwood, Lancashire FY7 6EU. If you haven't worked as a dental nurse before, telephone the National Examination Board on (01253) 778 417.

Doctors

Doctors are not permitted to work using the working holiday visa so they must be using another permit or have employer sponsorship. There is plenty of work available as a locum either within the NHS or with private hospitals and clinics. Doctors must register with the British Medical Council in order to be able to practice. Contact the Council at 78 Great Portland Street, London W1N 6JE. Tel: (0171) 580 7642. Enquire about both full and partial registration. There are jobs throughout the UK and agencies exist to place doctors in a range of hospitals and practices. Doctors working locums are in peak demand during the summer period and over Christmas. It is best to have full registration and some experience before going to the UK. Doctors can expect to earn about £15 per hour while consultants can get £30 and over per hour.

Nurses

Like supply teaching, nursing through an agency is specifically allowed by the working holiday visa given the shortage of nurses. To begin nursing in the UK you'll need to organise registration and this is done through the UK Central Council for Nursing, Midwifery and Health Visiting. Contact the council before you leave home as it can take two to three months to process your application and it will cost £70 for the application and £56 for registration for three years. Applicants with a Comprehensive Nursing Certificate or an Applied Science Diploma or degree need 12 months experience in general, mental health, mental handicap or paediatric nursing. Registered general or general and obstetric nurses should have three months general nursing experience but other requirements may also apply. There is work to be found in both NHS and private hospitals, nursing homes, clinics and general practice. Pay rates are set by the government and start at about £8-10 per hour. Higher rates are available for those with specialist skills such as intensive care. You will need at least two referees.

Occupational therapists

As there is a shortage of qualified staff, work is available for occupational therapists (OTs), and you shouldn't have to wait too long for a position. As usual it is best to use an agency who will be able to advise you on a range of issues. In order to work you'll need to be registered with the Council for Professions Supplementary to Medicine, Park House, 184 Kennington Park Road, London SE11. Tel: (0171) 582 0866. This process is not cheap: it costs £150 for your qualifications to be assessed and another £110 for a written assessment. If you get through this process registration will cost £17. You should begin this process before leaving home as the registration process can take a couple of months. OTs will find work in the hospital system providing therapy to those with learning or other difficulties. Rates of pay vary from £10-15 per hour or about £500 per week depending on your experience.

Pharmacists

Australian and New Zealand pharmacy qualifications are recognised in the UK and registration requires a four-week supervised pre-registration process along with membership of the Royal Pharmaceutical Society, 1 Lambeth High Street, London SE1. Tel: (0171) 735 9141. Fax: (0171) 735 7629. Membership of the society costs £125 per year and you should have at least one years experiencc in your home country. Most positions are available in hospitals, which is useful as many hospitals provide accommodation with the position. It is possible to find positions in locations outside London and going through an agency is the best bet for organising work. Experienced pharmacists can expect to earn the equivalent of about £30-35,000 per year.

Physiotherapists

There is a shortage of qualified and experienced physiotherapists throughout the UK so positions can be found throughout the country. The working holiday visa regulations specifically allow physiotherapists exemption from the 'no career work' rule. It is best to work through agencies as they can provide a good introduction to the field and often provide better pay. You'll need to register with the Council for Professions Supplementary to Medicine, Park House, 184 Kennington Park Road, London SE11. Tel: (0171) 582 0866. The registration process will take up to two months so you need to begin before you leave home. Pay rates vary from £10-15 per hour depending on experience.

Social workers

Both qualified and unqualified social workers will be able to find work through the appropriate agencies. The work is similar to that at home but the different rules and working environment can make the support provided by agencies very important. Some agencies will provide additional training to get up to scratch with appropriate legislation and, where needed, counselling. You will need to register with the Central Council for Education and Training at Derbyshire House, St Chad's Street, London WC1H 8AD. Tel: (0171) 278 2454. This process should begin before you leave home to allow it to be completed for your arrival in the UK. In any case you will require a police clearance and so you should visit your local police station to organise this. Pay for qualified social workers is about £9-10 per hour. Pay for unqualified social workers, who will find work as carers in homes or in residential institutions, is about £5 per hour.

Hospitality and tourism

Hospitality work picks up in September after university and college students have gone back to study, leaving behind many vacancies across a wide range of occupations, particularly in London. As Christmas looms closer end-of-year parties become more common, creating more demand for short-term jobs.

Cafes and restaurants

The UK is always full of tourists, about 17 million visit each year and most spend some time in central London. That's about 46,000 extra bodies on the street on an average day. And as they all want to eat and drink there is plenty of work in cafes, restaurants and hotels. If you are interested in a cafe, pick a favourite, walk in and ask. It's not unusual for notices advertising vacancies to be found on shopfronts. Experience in pouring a decent cappuccino will help get you behind the servery. You'll also find ads for hospitality positions in newspapers and magazines. Pay will be about £3-5 per hour plus tips. You should find out what the policy is on tips, i.e. do you keep your own or pool them with other staff at the end of each shift. If you are interested in classier work like silver service, and have some experience, then there are agencies catering to this need.

Cooking and catering

Catering includes work for chefs, other kitchen staff and the range of staff required for function catering. Chefs need some experience, the more up-market the establishment the more experience will be needed. Flashier establishments requiring more experienced or specialist chefs will also pay higher rates, up to £8-9 per hour. There is plenty of kitchen work around central London including meal preparation and dish washing, with these jobs paying around £3 per hour. Function catering outfits and agencies will require proof of experience and some references.

Fast food

If you're young enough and have some experience at McDonalds, KFC or Pizza Hut then these type of fast food outlets are littered across the UK and may be attractive to some.

Holiday activities

The oncoming summer sees a rapid growth in holiday centres and sporting activities and with this comes a great many jobs in a wide range of positions, both skilled and unskilled. These centres include holiday camps, activity centres, theme parks, outdoor recreation centres and riding schools. While pay for unskilled positions may not be high—it may only be about £40 per week—you'll usually get food and board as part of the job, along with a great time. Positions requiring qualifications and experience will command higher pay, but usually nothing outstanding as many of these positions can be filled by university and college students who are in the process of gaining additional work experience. Positions in these types of operations can include managerial, administrative, retail and catering staff, cleaners, childminders, activity organisers and attendants, a wide range of sports instructors, and counsellors. Recruitment for these positions begins long before summer, so you'll need to get in early. *Summer Jobs*, an annual publication from Vacation Work, is a good reference for tracking down potential employers.

Hotels

There is a vast number of positions inside a big hotel, ranging from working in the laundry to night manager, and everything in between. The multitude of hotels in London only adds to opportunities. If you plan to find some work in these hotels you'll have a better chance if you have some experience back home and maybe some qualifications, depending on what you are aiming at. During summer, hotels all over the UK take on extra staff to cater for the holiday rush and this could allow you to experience life in the country away from the rush of the metropolis.

Pubs

Bar work is a good standby and probably the most common work for antipodeans in the UK. It is relatively easy to get and can be found in one of the thousands of drinking establishments scattered throughout the UK. The disadvantages are that you may be working most nights and the hours can be long. The upside is the great social environment that most pubs will offer. You'll find both 'live-in' and 'live-out' positions, depending on which suits you, though many live-in arrangements will usually be in the more distant London suburbs or outside London altogether. Pay will vary from about £3-5 per hour (plus tips) depending on whether accommodation and meals are part of the deal and how much experience you have. If you're looking at this type of work take black trousers or skirts and white shirts or blouses as this is a pretty universal outfit. If you can pour a decent beer then you'll be fine; if not, then plenty of publicans are prepared to have you learn on the job. Some experience at home is a bonus even if you have to offer your services for free during slow times so you can see the world from the other side of the bar. Remember that in the UK what we call beer is called larger, and both are served at room temperature, and that Guinness is poured in two goes and no more.

Ski fields

There is only one ski area in the UK and that is around Glencoe in Scotland. The ski season runs from November to May, depending on the condition of the snow, and like most ski resorts, a wide range of staff is required. This includes on-snow staff such as lift operators and maintenance crew members and skiing instructors, in addition to staff to work in the retail areas, accommodation facilities and catering outlets. You can access work through ads in newspapers and magazines, through the employment agencies in the Highlands or by approaching the operators directly. However, remember that even by Australian and New Zealand standards these are small resorts with limited employment opportunities.

Travel consultants

Not surprisingly travel consulting work is seasonal with most temporary and contract work available in the build up to the summer holidays and through the summer period. Outside of this time you will most likely be filling in for unavailable staff. Those with qualifications (mainly Sabre and Galileo reservations systems), and agency and travel experience will be first in line for positions. Most positions will have a base salary of about £200 per week plus a commission of about 10%. Most work is in London. As with other types of work, there are also specialist agencies for placing travel consultants.

Youth hostels

During the summer period assistant wardens are taken on by many of the 320 or so youth hostels that are scattered throughout the UK, many in glorious rural locations. You'll need to apply early in the calendar year as some assistant wardens begin work as early as March and April, and you'll need to have a personal interview as part of the selection process. Contact YHA Recruitment, 8 St Stephen's Hill, St Albans, Herts, AL1 2DY for an application form. Check the *YHA Guide for England and Wales* and the separate publication *Scotland's Hostels* for contact details of the hostels.

Information technology (IT)

If there is one field of employment that has gone crazy it has to be information technology and telecommunications. Worldwide there are far more IT positions than there are people to fill them and the UK is no exception. All countries are putting rules and incentives in place in an attempt to attract IT workers (including Australia and New Zealand). With the rapid growth of IT, the looming millennium bug (and its aftermath) and in the case of Europe, the phasing in of the euro, there is no shortage of work. It is best to work through an agency for a contract position for which at least two years experience is necessary. The experience is often more important than the qualifications. There are a number of agencies that can begin the process in Australia and New Zealand, though you'll need to finalise any arrangements in the UK. However, there are always plenty of ads in newspapers and magazines in the UK, including those catering to travellers from down-under. You'll most likely need to sit a test to prove your stated abilities, but once you have established yourself at an agency you won't be short of work which usually pays upward of £400 per week. The skills required cover the broad spectrum of IT including network administration and support, programming, project management, administration and training. Experience with SAP/R3, Oracle 7, Visual Basic, Netware 3.x/4.1 and Lotus notes are sought after.

Legal

The similarity between the legal systems of the UK, Australia and New Zealand allows down-under lawyers and solicitors to work in the UK. There are a number of agencies specialising in this area. Lawyers can plan on earning about £9-30 per hour depending on the work.

Secretarial and office administration

Offices in the City of London in particular have an insatiable demand for those with the skills and experience that allow the administrative processes to run smoothly. This includes secretarial personnel, managers and administrative clerks of all types. Working through agencies is one way to go and there are many specialising in this area. A good knowledge of Microsoft applications (mostly Word, Excel and Powerpoint) is a prerequisite but an understanding of operating systems (mostly Windows 95) and sometimes other applications like WordPerfect and Word Pro (Ami Pro) along with Lotus 1-2-3 can be very useful. Secretaries will be expected to type about 80 wpm and having shorthand experience will sometimes be useful. Your skills and experience will determine whether you will be eligible for a more organisational role or more likely to end up in a typing position. Junior office assistants who undertake tasks like filing and photocopying (photostating in the UK) can expect to earn around £4-6 per hour. Clerical work pays around £6 per hour. Trained secretaries can get about £8-9 per hour while senior secretaries can earn about £8-11 per hour. Legal secretaries working as temps can expect a slightly higher salary, about £10-13 per hour.

Trades

Short-term contract work is available for a wide range of trades including carpenters, electricians, painters, plumbers, shopfitters and welders. Contracts may only last for a week or two but there are several agencies that specialise in this area so work can be continuous. Make sure you mail your qualifications to friends or to your poste restante address as you'll need these at agencies or when approaching potential employers. You'll also find ads in daily newspapers particularly *The Evening Standard*. You should consider having some of your most important tools with you for short-term contract work but don't take these with you, send them separately. Otherwise pick up some secondhand tools in London, often available at markets. Earnings begin at about £6-7 per hour.

Everything else

While this chapter has attempted to cover some of the more common positions taken by antipodeans in the UK there are a great many more jobs out there. These include call centre operators, cleaners, couriers, desktop publishers, factory workers, fork lift drivers, gym instructors, hairdressers, journalists (see Jeannie Zakharov's story), labourers, medical technicians, security agents, storemen and shop assistants (especially in the lead up to Christmas and at sale times), to name only some. Vacancies in many of these areas can be found in newspapers and magazines but there are also specialist agencies for just about all of these jobs. Fork lift drivers, who require a licence for either a reach truck or a counterbalance truck and with appropriate qualifications, and some experience, can expect to earn about £500 per week. Couriers are also in demand, especially at busy times of the year like Christmas, whether delivering by van, motorcycle or bicycle. Most of the delivery work around the West End is done by bicycle couriers. Courier companies welcome enquiries, especially from experienced motorcycle riders, with training for London conditions being provided by the company. Payment is based on the number of deliveries you make, but once you get the hang of London you could expect to earn at least £350 per week. Bicycle couriers earn less.

Not mentioned so far is the North Sea oil and gas industry, based in Aberdeen, in part because opportunities here peaked some time back and with the current state of the industry (low oil prices and limited exploration) jobs are probably in decline. That's not to say that those with a knowledge of and experience in the industry couldn't find work there.

There are no doubt plenty of other jobs that people have found by good fortune or because they pursued a particular passion. You don't have to stick to the beaten path!

Kids schooled in AFL

Murray Hedgcock

When the West Coast Eagles were victorious over Collingwood in the AFL exhibition match at The Oval, London last year, the most rewarding segment of play was at halftime.

As expatriates surged onto the famous turf of The Oval for the traditional kick-to-kick, tiny figures in Eagle and Magpie guernseys took up position on their section of the ground, with adults setting up temporary goalposts.

To the delight and generous applause of the 11,500-strong crowd, the boys, and girls, of Wheatfield Junior School played their hearts out in a unique display of the great Aussie game.

Controlling the exercise as field umpire, restraining the more vigorous and encouraging the less forceful, was the man behind the match, teacher Eugene 'Euey' Lee, originally from the tiny Victorian town of Wangoon, just outside Warrnambool.

Lee, now 36, admits to being a moderate halfback in a very moderate students' team, the Warrnambool Sharks, and with local club Coolbinia-Yokine in Perth before turning to umpiring. He taught at Sacred Heart Primary, Highgate; John XXIII College, Mount Claremont; and St Denis Joondanna Primary School before coming to Britain on a teacher exchange.

In just three months of once-a-week after-school coaching, Euey Lee has made the Australian code something special at this 380-pupil school in St Ives, a Cambridgeshire market town of 15,000 people, 100 kilometres north of London.

'We arrived just after Christmas; moving from 44 degrees to minus two degrees,' he recalls. (The family has grown since arriving, wife Kate and two-year-old daughter Grace joined by three-month-old Evelyn.)

'Wheatfields runs after-school clubs, where children can try anything from sewing to soccer; they pay £1.50 (about $3.50) and the money is spent on school amenities.

'The headmaster, the only other male teacher on the staff of a dozen, agreed I could try Aussie Rules, and we had 22 turn up regularly last term for the first 10 weeks, with about 38 since the new school year began in September.'

The aim is to make it fun, not fiercely competitive, with sessions devoted to special skills: kicking, marking, handball and so on. The children are aged seven to 10, and girls join in.

'No-one had ever seen it played, although AFL games are seen here on Sky satellite TV, but we started with one football I had brought over, and the AFL sent us more.

'There was a lot of leg-pulling but no-one objected to introducing the code, not even in a country where soccer has such a hold. When I saw about the Eagles match I contacted the organisers, and they agreed to allow the children to play, too.'

The English remain wary of this alien code; The Oval's groundsman hastily goes on holiday before footy hits his beloved turf, and the Surrey CCC vetoed the idea of the St Ives match as a curtain-raiser, worried that the little chaps would tear up the ground before the main event.

On the big day a convoy of 100 parents, teachers and children made the trek to town—many of the children never having been to London—with Euey warm in his thanks to colleagues who gave up a precious day off.

Small guernseys donated by the AFL were waiting. All 42 recruits turned out, with their mini-oval divided into three zones, the teams split into groups and rotated from defence to midfield to attack after five minutes, to ensure that everyone got a chance. Tackling was strictly limited; once touched, a player had three seconds to dispose of the ball.

Lee was so busy ensuring everyone got a fair go that he forgot to check his stop-watch, and was set to allow play to continue when he found his colleagues had removed the posts and were running off, as the big teams were about to return. But there was time for the youngsters to do a lap of honour, getting enormous applause from a sporting crowd.

There were delightful scenes at the end when the little blokes, still proudly sporting their guernseys, got autographs and had photos taken with the AFL stars, who behaved just right with their small admirers.

Back at St Ives the next day, the West Coast Eagles song was played over the school amplifying system, the players were allowed to wear their treasured guernseys for the week, instead of school uniform, and there have been more playground Aussie Rules games than soccer, says Euey Lee with much pleasure.

'It really does have benefits; slightly timid girls can now be seen standing up for their rights (they went barging through the boys at The Oval), and everyone seems to gain in confidence. When I go home to Perth at Christmas, there are hopes that a couple of the women teachers will carry on with the game.'

Who won the kids' match? Slight problem; as the goal umpires had never done the job before, and had to be hastily instructed en route to London, no-one actually knows. And no-one cares, because this was one game of Aussie Rules where it was playing, not winning, that truly mattered.

Finding work

Bryan Havenhand

If you haven't begun to organise work before leaving home then starting from scratch in the UK is no great problem, provided you have all the necessary paperwork. This includes a police clearance if you intend to work with children as a teacher or social worker. This chapter provides information on both temporary and permanent work, although the conditions of your visa will determine what sort of work you are able to pursue. The focus is on London simply because this is where most work is found and because most antipodeans end up working in London, at least for part of their time in the UK. However, there are numerous opportunities outside London and while many occupations will have the same pay rates throughout the UK, living costs outside London can be up to 25% lower.

The ad hoc approach

You can be lucky, no doubt about it: someone knows of a job, someone's leaving a job, you were the first to see a great job ad pinned on the hostel noticeboard or you saw a position advertised in an office window. It happens! But if luck doesn't come your way then there are many other paths to choose when it comes to looking for a job.

Newspapers and magazines

There is no shortage of newspapers and magazines in London or the UK in general. To start with there are the daily quality newspapers: *The Daily Telegraph* (//telegraph.co.uk), *The Guardian* (//guardian.co.uk), *The Times* (//the-times.co.uk), *The Independent* and *The Financial Times*. Like similar newspapers in Australia and New Zealand these papers are the most useful for employment advertisements. *The Guardian* has a 'Jobs and Money' section each Saturday listing a full range of jobs. The main tabloids, the *Daily Express*, the *Daily Mail*, the *Mirror* and the *Sun*, are less useful. *The Evening Standard* is the only evening daily in London. It has lots of jobs in Friday's classifieds, and on Monday it has a 'Just the Job' section. *Loot* (www.loot.com) is a daily 'Free-Ads' newspaper that has a small employment section but a large accommodation section.

There are weeklies available from newsagents including *Jobs and Careers Weekly* and *Job Hunters Guide*. If you are heading to Scotland you'll find *Scottish Jobs* and *Scottish Recruitment*. There are a number of free weeklies aimed at the large antipodean and South Afrian population in London and these are an excellent source of employment advertising. The best by far is the *TNT Magazine* (www.tntmag.co.uk) though there are a numbr of others (in rough order of usefulness for jobs ads) including *New Zealand News UK* (www.nznewsuk.co.uk), *The Star* and *SA Times*, *Southern Cross* (www.southerncorss.co.uk) and *LAM*. *TNT Magazine* comes out on Mondays and is in high demand so you'll need to get in early to get one from the yellow dump bins at major Underground stations. Other free weeklies with job ads aimed more at Londoners in general including *Nine to Five* (www.londoncareers.net) and *Ms London* (www.londoncareers.net). *Big Issue*, sold on the streets by the homeless for £1, has some positions, usually for social change organisations. *The Lady*, available in newsagents, is worth looking at if you are after domestic positions such as nannies and carers or positions in hospitality.

There is a wide range of magazines aimed at particular professions such as *Caterer and Hotelkeeper*, *Professional Nurse*, *Nursing Times* and *Nursery World*, all found in newsagents and with plenty of employment advertising. Other specialist periodicals also exist, some of these are found in newsagents and others in specialist bookshops. Professional associations produce their own publications for members so you may wish to make contact with the professional association to which you could belong. If you are a member of your association at home, some benefits may exit in the UK for you.

The Internet

Despite what is written in the daily press, finding international jobs independently over the Internet requires some net savvy which not everyone has (yet) and is most common in the IT industries, which is not really surprising. Most positions will still require a face-to-face interview before a job is confirmed. One UK-based site aimed specifically at Australians and New Zealanders that advertises more than 3000 UK job vacancies each week in the IT, business and finance sectors is www.jobworld.co.uk.

Where available, website addresses have been included throughout this book and they are a good place to begin a search for information about jobs, if only as a point of comparison between agencies. The *TNT Magazine* site, www.tntmag.co.uk, has a 'Word of Mouth' section which usually has plenty of ads for jobs, mostly for those in which qualifications are less important, such as pub work and courier positions.

Books

There are a few books available down-under that may be of use. One in particular is an annual publication from Vacation Press in the UK called *Summer Jobs Britain* which should be available through most bookshops. See the appendix for details.

'Teaching in Scotland' is a kit prepared by Janine Mergler who wanted to teach in Scotland on a working holiday visa but found it difficult to do so. Agencies were not interested in Scottish schools and so Scottish schools were not interested in temporary and contract teachers from down-under. Janine eventually fought her way through the bureaucratic paperwork and found teaching positions in Scotland. Not only did she have a great time but in order to make it easier for those from down-under who might be interested in teaching in Scotland, she has put together this package. It includes all the necessary documents and other information required for applying for teaching positions in Scotland. Send $25 to Teaching in Scotland, 36 Craig Street,

Brighton Qld 4017 to receive your copy or telephone (07) 3269 3804 for more details.

Jobcentres

The Jobcentre is the government job finding agency and by holding a legitimate work visa you are eligible to use these offices to find work. Some of these offices, mostly in London, have a Temporary Desk. However, as a foreigner, you won't always receive a warm welcome so it's best to stick to those agencies that cater for antipodeans and know the rules.

Agencies

Using employment agencies is the easiest way to go when looking for a position but it's not a one-way street. For an agency to do the best for you and keep you supplied with work, especially during the slower times of the year, you'll need to contribute in terms of adequate preparation and by cooperating with the agency. Don't wait for the agency to contact you, you'll need to ring daily when you are ready to work. Make sure you get to know someone by name so you'll be recognised when you call. It's a big field, with some 63,000 consultants placing about 900,000 people in temporary positions throughout the UK each year. Placing temporary employees in positions is over 90% of the work of recruitment agencies.

The agencies included here are only intended to be a sample of the vast number in the UK (not all of whom are interested in catering to antipodeans). In most cases the London contact is given as it is often the head office. The agencies listed below are keen to have antipodeans on their list of available employees or contractors. Australian and/or New Zealand addresses are given where possible and where it is understood that the local office will actively promote your case to the UK office. A few agencies listed here are able to place you in a position before you arrive in the UK. If a local office refers you onto their UK office, make sure you get specific details about who to see and what to expect. The author knows of a couple of cases in which working holiday-makers approached a local office of a recruitment firm and were referred in glowing terms to the UK office only to arrive at the office in London as unknowns. Needless to say they felt very let down—not a good start to their stay in the UK. In most cases you won't be guaranteed a position until you have a face-to-face interview in the UK.

The recruitment agencies are listed alphabetically and cross referenced as many agencies recruit for several occupational groups. Make contact with the local office first as they may be able to begin the process by sending your file to their UK office. If you are a teacher, definitely contact the local office first. Otherwise, contact the UK office direct, letting them know who you are by sending your CV as well as your plans for working in the UK including when you'll be arriving.

Please note that before contacting the agencies listed below, you must ensure that you are eligible to work in the UK either by having a working holiday visa, a visa based on patriality or ancestry or by holding a British or another European Union country passport, or by haveing a spouse who meets the last criteria if they also reside in the UK. In the last case you'll still need to apply for a work visa. You may be able to obtain employer sponsorship but in most cases you would need to deal directly with the employer. There are some occasions in which employer sponsorship can be organised through a recruitment agency but only in highly sought after occupations, namely IT positions and some teaching and nursing positions. Such employer sponsorship is job specific.

Job agencies by occupational group

Accounting, banking and finance: Australasian Temp Company, Bligh Appointments, Hays Personnel Services, Hewitson-Walker, Martin Ward Anderson, Michael Page International, Morgan and Banks, Robert Half/Accountemps, Target Appointments, Walker Hamill.

Agriculture: Bligh Appointments, Fletcher Relief Services, Target Appointments.

Domestic positions: Bligh Appointments, Koala Nannies.

Education and teaching: ASA Education, BMG Associates, Initial Education Personnel, LHR Education, Quality Teachers, Spring Education, Teach UK, Teacher Employment Network, Timeplan.

Engineering and construction: Eden Brown, Euro Elite, Hays Personnel Services, Euro Personnel Services.

Healthcare: BMG Associates, Countryside Medical Selection, Elite Recruitment Specialists, European Nursing Agency, IPA Healthcare, Medi Placements, Nightingale Nursing Bureau, Nursing Management Services, Premier Nursing.

Hospitality and tourism: Abbey Recruitment, Dee Cooper, Travel Jobshops.

Information technology: Computer Consultants International, Cowdell McNally Consulting, Eurolink Consulting, Hays Personnel Services, Interpro CRI, Lester Associates, Rimpac, Walker Hamill.

Legal: Garfield Robbins International, Learned Friends, Mahlab Recruitment, Taylor Root.

Printing and publishing: Australasian Temp Company, Dagmar Tara.

Sales, marketing and call centres: Stop the Gap Marketing, KLR Personnel.

Retail: Target Appointments.

Secretarial and office administration: Australasian Temp Company, Bligh Appointments, Eden Brown, Learned Friends, Verity Appointments.

Unskilled work: Bligh Appointments.

Job agencies - contact details

Abbey Recruitment

18 James Street, London W1M 5HN.

Tel: (0171) 495 4342. Fax: (0171) 495 4345.

Email: enquiries@abbeyrecuitment.co.uk.

Website: www.abbeyrecruitment.co.uk.

Recruits experienced staff for hospitality and catering positions including chefs, restaurant managers, food and beverage staff and receptionists.

ASA Education

Glade House, 52 Carter Lane, London EC4V 5EA.

Tel: (0171) 329 4777. Fax: (0171) 329 4997.

PO Box 7505, Cloisters Square, Perth WA 6850.

Tel: (08) 9480 3736. Fax: (08) 9321 3531.

Recruits teachers for relief, contract and permanent positions in London and south eastern England.

Australasian Temp Company

128-129 Cheapside, London EC2V 6BT.

Tel: (0171) 600 1709. Fax: (0171) 600 2133.

Email: enquiries@australasian-temps.co.uk.

Website: www.australasian-temps.co.uk.

with **Lampen Group**

Level 1, BHP House, 1 Castlereagh Street, Sydney NSW 2000.

Tel: (02) 9221 0900. Fax: (02) 9221 0500.

Email: lampen@tmx.com.au.

16th Floor, Stock Exchange Bldg, Queen Street, Auckland.

Tel: (09) 357 9800. Fax: (09) 357 9801

Email: auckland@lampen.co.nz.

Recruit secretaries, desktop publishing operators, receptionists, administrators, banking operations clerks, accounts staff, and VDU/data entry operators.

Bligh Appointments

131-135 Earls Court Road, London SW5 9RH.

Tel: (0171) 244 7277.

Email: bligh.appointments@binternet.com.

Level 7, Dymocks Bldg, 428 George Street, Sydney NSW 2000.

Tel: (02) 9235 3699. Fax: (02) 9221 3480.

Email: bligh@real.net.au.

An Australian company specialising in placing Australians and New Zealanders in a range of jobs including accountants, secretaries, data entry operators, WP operators, clerks, nannies, mothers' helps, farm workers and labourers.

BMG Associates

PO Box 2304, Fitzroy MDC Vic 3065.

Tel: (03) 9416 2333. Toll free: 1800 677 948 (for medical positions) and 1800 813 149 (for teachers). Fax: (03) 9416 2399.

Email: info@bmgassociates.com.au.

Website: www.bmgassociates.com.au.

61 Malvern Road, Mount Albert, Auckland 1003.

Tel/Fax: 0800 803 854.

Recruits audiologists, medical scientists, operating theatre staff, occupational therapists, pharmacists, physiotherapists, speech pathologists and social workers for locum and contract positions throughout the UK. Also recruits, on behalf of Teachers UK, primary and secondary teachers for short-term and longer term contract teaching positions throughout the UK.

Computer Consultants International

PO Box 82, East Horsley, Leatherhead KT24 5YY.

Tel: (01483) 280 060.

Website: www.cciuk.com.

PO Box 1284, Collingwood Vic 3066.

Tel: (03) 9416 3377. Fax: (03) 9419 5620.

Email: staff@cca-cci.net. Website: www.cca.com.au.

PO Box 5467, Wellington.

Tel: (04) 473 8597. Fax: (04) 473 8580.

Email: cate@cci.co.nz. Website: www.cci.co.nz

Recruits all positions within the IT industry, permanent and contract. CCI handles everything required for relocation: visas, flights, initial accommodation, information on your destination and client briefing. Ongoing contact and support for contractors offered.

Countrywide Medical Selection

Eastgate House, Eastgate Street, Winchester, Hants S023 8D2.

Tel: (0171) 636 1810. Fax: (0171) 636 1910.

Email: cms@cms-ltd.co.uk.

19 Girraman Street, Chermside West Qld 4032.

Tel/Fax: (07) 3350 3992.

Email: pippacms@powerup.com.au.

Recruits occupational therapists for locum, contract and permanent positions throughout the UK.

Cowdell McNally Consulting

Level 10, CML Bldg, 14 Martin Place, Sydney NSW 2000.

Tel: (02) 9221 4999. Fax: (02) 9221 4199.

Email: resume@cmcaust.com.

Recruits all positions within the IT industry, permanent and contract. Works with Compucare and Best People in the UK.

Dagmar Tara

48 Chandos Place, London WC2N 4HS.

Tel: (0171) 379 4141.

Recruits for a range of positions in the printing and desktop publishing industry. Positions require a minimum of two years experience.

Dee Cooper

Tel: (01764) 670 001/679 728.

Recruits waiting, bar, house and kitchen staff wanting live-in positions (only) in hotels and pubs throughout the UK. Dee Cooper can find positions for singles, couples and sometimes groups of travellers.

Eden Brown

2 Plough Yard, London EC2A 3LP.

Tel: (0171) 377 6222. Fax: (0171) 377 1313.

Recruits occupational groups in three main areas (experience required): secretarial, architectural, and civil, mechanical and electrical engineering.

Elite Recruitment Specialists

20 Grosvenor Place, Belgravia, London SWIX 7HN.

Free phone: (800) 235 19000. Free fax: (800) 235 17000.

Email: recruit@elitemedical.co.uk.

Brisbane

Tel: (07) 3358 2600.

Wellington

Tel: (04) 476 7342. Fax: (04) 476 3048.

Recruits across the range of medical positions including doctors, pharmacists, physiotherapists, occupational therapists, speech and language therapists, social workers and audiologists for placement throughout the UK.

European Nursing Agency

113 Victoria Street, St Albans

Tel: (01727) 850 600.

Recruits experienced carers and nursing staff for home-based care in and around London.

Eurolink Consulting

Eurolink House, 41 Tamworth Road, Croydon CR0 1XU

Toll free 0808 100 4000. Fax: (0181) 649 9214.

Email: london@eurolink-consulting.co.uk.

Website: www.eurolink-consulting.co.uk.

Level 7, 333 George Street, Sydney NSW 2000.

Tel: (02) 9262 6577. Fax: (02) 9262 6701.

Email: jobs@eurolink.com.au. Website: www.eurolink.com.au.

Recruits all positions within the IT industry,throughout the UK, permanent and contract, by putting you in contact with the UK office.

Euro Elite

Western Australian House, 113-116 The Strand, London WC2R 0AA

Tel: (0171) 240 4440. Fax: (0171) 379 7208.

Email: recruit@euroelite.co.uk. Website: www.euroelite.co.uk.

PO Box 1363, Hastings, New Zealand.

Tel: (06) 877 4174.

Email: bert.selles@clear.net.nz.

Recruits engineers and technicians, from technical support positions through to project engineers, across a range of industries. Permanent, temporary and contract positions with consultants, contractors and local authorities. An information pack is available from their New Zealand address, above.

Euro Personnel Services

10th Floor, Cannon Centre, 78 Cannon Street, London EC4N 6HH.

Tel: (0171) 623 0101.

Recruits a wide range of occupations for the building industry including electricians, mechanical fitters, heating and combustion engineers, trade assistants, and air conditioning and refrigeration mechanics.

Fletcher Relief Services

Fieldside Farm, Quainton nr Aylesbury, Bucks HP22 4DQ.

Tel: (01296) 655 777. Fax: (01296) 655 779.

Recruits those with three years experience to provide relief work on farms throughout the UK. Farms include dairy, beef, sheep, pigs and cropping. Free board and lodgings.

Garfield Robbins International

2 Wormwood Street, London EC2M 1RQ.

Tel: (0171) 417 1400. Fax: (0171) 417 1444.

Level 29, Chifley Tower, 2 Chifley Square, Sydney NSW 2000.

Tel: (02) 9375 2181. Fax: (02) 9375 2185.

Recruits qualified lawyers for private practice and industry throughout the UK.

Hays Personnel Services

London

Tel: (0171) 588 4244.

Website: www.hays.co.uk.

GPO Box 3868, Sydney NSW 2001.

Tel: (02) 9229 7113. Fax: (02) 9221 4347.

Hays Personnel Services, like many large recruiting agencies, covers many occupational groups. In Australia telephone (02) 9229 7113 for finance and banking, customer service, administration and legal work; telephone (02) 9249 2200 for occupations involved in construction work and telephone (02) 9229 7198 for IT work. Staff at all these Sydney telephone numbers are able to link you to Hays' offices in the UK.

Hewitson-Walker

New Zealand House, 80 Haymarket, London SW1Y 4HW.

Tel: (0171) 321 2999. Fax: (0171) 839 5919.

Email: info@hewitson-walker.co.uk.

Website: www.hewitson-walker.co.uk.

with **Recruitment Solutions**

Sydney.

Tel: (02) 9377 9666.

Email: syd@recruitment-solutions.com.au.

Website: www.recruitment-solutions.com.au.

and **Opal Consulting**

Auckland.

Tel: (09) 379 0200.

Email: mackey@opalconsult.co.nz. Website: www.opalconsult.co.nz.

Recruit professionals in general and specialist accounting fields for temporary, contract and permanent positions. Recruitment Solutions and Opal Consulting work with Hewitson-Walker in London.

Initial Education Personnel

London.

Tel: (0171) 645 5101.

PO Box 272, Fremantle WA 6160.

Tel: (08) 9335 3229. Mobile: 041 147 0858. Fax: (08) 9335 4470.

Recruits teachers for nursery, primary, secondary and special needs schools for daily and contract positions throughout London, Birmingham and Leeds.

InterPRO

99-101 Farrington Road, London EC1R 3BT.

Tel: (0171) 689 1461. Fax: (0171) 689 4876.

PO Box Q609 QVB, Sydney NSW 1230.

Tel: (02) 9283 3555. Fax: (02) 9283 3634.

Email: resume@interpro.com.au. Website: www.interpro.com.au.

Recruits for all positions within the IT industry for contract and permanent positions.

IPA Heathcare

Level 12, 440 Collins Street, Melbourne Vic 3000.

Tel: (03) 9252 2272. Fax: (03) 9670 4984.

Email: healthcare@ipagroup.com.au/health.htm.

Recruits nurses, doctors, physiotherapists, occupational therapists and pharmacists for temporary, contract, locum and permanent positions in various work environments including hospitals and health clinics throughout the UK.

KLR Personnel

2nd Floor, 42-43 Lower Marsh, London SE1 7RG.

Tel: (0171) 928 5111. Fax: (0171) 928 5070.

Email: recruitment@klr.co.uk.

Recruits call centre and customer service staff at all levels up to senior management. You need to have a good telephone manner and a good knowledge of MS Office.

Koala Nannies

22 Craven Terrace, London W2.

Tel: (0171) 402 4224. Fax: (0171) 706 7202.

Email: koala_nannies@compuserve.com.

Recruits nannies for live-in and live-out positions.

Learned Friends

Bride House, 18-20 Bride Lane, London EC4Y 8DX.

Tel: (0171) 583 5955. Fax: (0171) 583 5966.

Level 7, 92 Pitt Street, Sydney NSW 2000.

Tel: (02) 9232 5858. Fax: (02) 9232 5875.

Email: lfs@learnedfr.com.au.

Level 5, 179 Queen Street, Melbourne Vic 3000.

Tel: (03) 9642 3992. Fax: (03) 9642 3994.

Email: ifmelb@learnedfr.com.au.

Recruits solicitors, paralegals, secretaries, receptionists and administration staff for temporary, contract and permanent positions in the legal, banking and finance, and accounting environments.

Lester Associates

2nd Floor, Broadway Chambers, 20 Hammersmith Broadway

London W6 7BB.

Tel: (0171) 413 3900. Fax: (0171) 413 3939.

Email: contractor.centre@lester-assoc.com.

PO Box 6138, North Sydney NSW 2060.

Tel: (02) 9956 8228. Fax: (02) 9956 8499.

Email: lester@lester.com.au. Website: www.lester.com.au.

An accounting firm specialising in taxation matters for IT contractors in addition to providing a job finding service for IT contractors in the UK, including employer sponsorship.

LHR Education

London.

Tel: (0181) 600 1300.

Email: teachers@lhr-ed.co.uk. Website: www.lhrteachers.co.uk.

PO Box 1032, Warrnambool Vic 3280.

Tel: (03) 5562 9426. Fax: (03) 5562 9426.

Email: lhr@standard.net.au.

Wellington.

Tel: (04) 387 2939.

Email: lhr@xtra.co.nz.

Recruits teachers for primary, secondary, pre-school and childcare staff in London and across to Wales for casual, day-to-day work and term contracts.

Mahlab Recruitment

Level 6, 20 Loftus Street, Sydney NSW 2000.

Tel: (02) 9241 1199. Fax: (02) 9241 1189.

Email: admin@mahlabrecruitment.com.au.

Website: www.mahlab.com.au.

Recruits lawyers for contract and permanent positions in conjunction with an associated office in London.

Martin Ward Anderson

7 Savoy Court, The Strand, London WC2R OEL.

Tel: (0171) 240 2233. Fax: (0171) 240 8818.

Email: info@mwa.co.uk. Website: www.mwa.co.uk.

Recruits personnel for accounting, IT and banking and finance positions in temporary, contract or permanent placements.

Medi Placements

874-880 Eastern Avenue, Ilford, Essex IG2 7HY.

Tel: (0181) 491 8899. Fax: (0181) 491 8999.

Recruits a wide range of positions including social workers, occupational therapists, physiotherapists, audiologists, speech and language therapists and cardiac technicians.

Michael Page International

London.

Tel: (0171) 831 2000. Fax: (0171) 329 2953.

Sydney.

Tel: (02) 9254 0255. Fax: (02) 9254 0201.

Auckland.

Tel: (09) 358 7110. Fax: (09) 358 7176.

Website: www.michaelpage.com.

Recruits accounting and financial personnel for placement in a range of working environments throughout the UK. A specialist division focuses on the needs of banking and financial institutions in the City of London, which includes filling positions in finance, operations, legal departments and IT.

Morgan and Banks

Brettenham House, Lancaster Place, London WC2N 7EN.

Tel: (0171) 240 1040. Fax: (0171) 240 1052.

Email: info@morganbanks.co.uk.

Level 11, Grosvenor Place, 205 George Street, Sydney NSW 2000.

Tel: (02) 9256 0333. Fax: (02) 9251 3975.

Email: info@morganbanks.com.au.

Website: www.morganbanks.com.au.

Level 6, Ports of Auckland Bldg, Quay Street, Auckland.

Tel: (09) 367 9000. Fax: (09) 367 9001.

Website: www.morganbanks.co.nz.

Recruits accountants and financial professionals for contract and permanent positions. If contracted with Morgan and Banks for more than 16 weeks you will be eligible for a Career Edge career guidance workshop upon return to Australia or New Zealand.

Nightingale Nursing Bureau

2 Tavistock Place, London WC1H 9RA.

Tel: (0171) 833 3952.

Sydney.

Tel: (02) 9878 8716.

Auckland.

Tel: (09) 623 1390.

Recruits nurses for short-term and long-term positions in a range of institutions.

Nursing Management Services

Level 1, 161 Walker Street, North Sydney NSW 2060.

Tel: (02) 9956 7533. Toll free: 1800 357 533. Fax: (02) 9956 7833.

Email: mail@nursingmanagementserv.com.au.

Website: www.citysearch.com.au/syd/nms.

New Zealand.

Toll free: 0800 445 582.

Recruits registered nurses for contracts ranging from 13 to 52 weeks at a variety of public and private hospitals throughout England.

Premiere Nursing

219 Kensington High Street, London W8 6BD.

Tel: (0171) 938 1977.

Email: nursing@premieregroup.co.uk.

Recruits registered nurses and experienced carers for work in London hospitals and for live-in or live-out home care positions.

Quality Teachers

9a High Street, Kings Heath, Birmingham B14 7BB.

Tel: (0121) 441 5121. Fax: (0121) 441 4959.

Email: geoff@quality-teachers.co.uk.

Website: www.quality-teachers.co.uk.

PO Box 536, Gymea NSW 2227.

Tel/Fax: (02) 9526 2855.

Recruits teachers for primary and secondary schools in Birmingham and the West Midlands for casual placement or longer term assignments. Wages are comparable with London but living costs are about 25% lower and the lifestyle is less stressful.

Rimpac

Atrium Court, Apex Plaza, Reading Berks RG1 1AX.

Tel: (01189) 254 225.

Email: rcsummers@compuserve.com. Website: www.rimpac.co.uk.

PO Box 1834, North Sydney NSW 2059.

Tel: (02) 9959 4889. Fax: (02) 9959 4358.

Email: it@rimpac.com.au.

Recruits all positions within the IT industry for permanent and contract work on clients' projects.

Robert Half/Accountemps

Walter House, 418 The Strand, London WC2R 0PT.

Tel: (0171) 395 9600. Fax: (0171) 836 4942.

Website: www.roberthalf.co.uk.

PO Box R428, Royal Exchange NSW 1224.

Tel: (02) 9241 6255. Fax: (02) 9241 6233.

Email: rhalf@rhi.aust.com

Recruits professionals in accountancy, and banking and finance, from account clerks to CEOs. Temporary accounting positions a speciality.

Spring Education

Teachers' Information Centre, London.

Tel: (0171) 629 4232.

Email: education@spring.com. Website: www.spring.com.

GPO Box 2132, Brisbane Qld 4001.

Tel: (07) 3231 0519. Fax: (07) 3211 2949.

133 West Tamaki Road, Glendowiotkl, Auckland.

Tel: (09) 521 3002. Fax: (09) 521 3004.

Recruits teachers for primary, secondary and special needs schools for contract and permanent positions.

Stop the Gap Marketing

Fitzroy House, 3 Paradise Road, Richmond, Surrey TW9 1RX.

Tel: (0181) 332 7656. Fax: (0181) 332 2747.

Recruits marketing people with two to three years experience in the areas of direct marketing, advertising, public relations, sales promotion, marketing communications, product management or market research.

Target Appointments

5th Floor, Sicilian House, Sicilian Avenue, London WC1A 2QH.

Tel: (0171) 242 1183. Fax: (0171) 405 5542.

Email: targettemp@aol.com.

Recruits for retail sales positions, both temporary and permanent, and for security personnel to work in a retail environment. Also recruits for accounting, banking and finance positions, landscape gardeners, labourers and horticulturist for work throughout the UK.

Taylor Root

179 Queen Victoria Street, London EC4V 4DD.

Tel: (0171) 415 2828.

Level 26, 1 O'Connell Street, Sydney NSW 2000.

Tel: (02) 9256 6670. Fax: (02) 9247 1957.

Email: suzietracey@taylor-root.com.au.

Recruits lawyers, solicitors and other legal personnel for contract and permanent positions.

Teach UK

PO Box 995, Rosny Park Tas 7018.

Tel: (03) 6244 8133. Fax: (03) 6244 5014.

Email: info@teachuk.com.au. Website: www.teachuk.com.au.

Recruits teachers for primary and secondary schools around London and southern England for contract positions. Teach UK is able to provide each successful applicant with a contract detailing their teaching assignment prior to their departure. Employer sponorship is also possible in some situations.

Teacher Employment Network

PO Box 1804, Toowong Qld 4066.

Tel: (07) 3371 4146. Fax: (07) 3371 6066.

Email: recruit@teacheremployment.com.au.

Website: www.teacheremployment.com.au.

Through Timeplan, recruits teachers for contract and permanent teaching positions in primary and secondary schools throughout the UK.

Timeplan

London

Tel: (0181) 371 8030.

Website: www.timeplan.com.

PO Box 903, Baulkham Hills NSW 2153.

Tel/Fax: (02) 9838 0148.

Email: jgroarke@activ.com.au. (Residents of NSW, ACT, NT and WA should use this NSW address.)

11 Commercial Road, Fortitude Valley Qld 4006.

Tel: (07) 3371 4146. Fax: (07) 3371 6066.

Email: ten@powerup.com.au. (Residents of Queensland should use this Qld address.)

89 Walkers Road, Mount Eliza Vic 3930.

Tel/Fax: (03) 9787 4606.

Email: richard@fox.net.au. (Residents of Victoria, SA and Tasmania should use this Vic address.)

Recruits teachers for short-term and long-term positions in primary and secondary schools throughout London.

Travel Jobshop

Level 4, 16 Mortimor Street, London W1N 7RD.

Tel: (0171) 580 2131. Fax: (0171) 580 1239.

Email: careers@traveljobshop.co.uk.

Website: www.traveljobshop.co.uk.

Recruits travel consultants with experience who are Galileo and Sabre trained for temporary and contract positions throughout the UK.

Verity Appointments

10 South Molton Street, Mayfair, London W1Y 1DF.

Tel: (0171) 493 0437. Fax: (0171) 493 0467.

Recruits legal secretaries for short-term and long-term placements.

Walker Hamill

103-105 Jermyn Street, St James, London SW1Y 6EE.

Tel: (0171) 839 4444. Fax: (0171) 976 1601.

Email: london@walker-hamill.co.uk.

Website: www.walkerhamill.com.

Level 39, Gateway, 1 Macquarie Place, Sydney NSW 2000.

Tel: (02) 9247 5655. Fax: (02) 9238 2336.

Email: australia@walker-hamill.co.uk.

Recruit accountants and IT professionals for temporary, contract and permanent positions.

Writing away

Jeannie Zakharov

Opting for London as a locale is not necessarily the most difficult option in terms of starting life in another country. The locals obviously speak English, and many of the television shows are familiar, as are brand names, and easily recognised Monopoly board place names are dotted across London Underground maps.

Despite the familiarity of the UK through historical and cultural ties—several centuries of literature, not to mention today's television shows, movies and music videos—starting out afresh in the UK still makes any foreigner realise how much of our daily life is spent on autodrive. On home territory we don't have to think about many of the mundane and myriad details that make up each day: how to buy train tickets and have them validated, how to register a car, order a beer in a pub, find a dentist or a doctor; even who to tip and how much. In one sense the foreigner is like a child again and has to learn how to do things that have long since become second nature at home, all in the absence of familiar support networks. You can no longer take your washing back to Mum and Dad's place. It's time to be resourceful!

This aspect of being a foreigner struck me even more forcefully in Amsterdam, where I lived for a couple of months before heading to London for work. I remember going to a supermarket on my first day, admittedly still jet lagged from my flight from Australia and feeling as disoriented as if I'd been woken at 3am. I realised I couldn't make head or tail of most of the products on display. Apart from a few familiar brands such as Coke and Moccona coffee, everything was in 'double Dutch' as far as I was concerned. How do I tell the difference between a packet of sugar and a packet of salt? What's the Dutch word for basil, or tarragon? Is that a carton of milk or a carton of yoghurt? The one easy choice was cheese, anything you like as long as it's gouda or edam. My sense of child-like disorientation in a strange place wasn't helped by the stature of the locals who crowded the aisles: Dutch people are tall and I felt like I was level with the average Amsterdam armpit.

Back to the other side of the North Sea. Once I'd seen a few of those London sites that pop up in old Michael Caine movies, learned to call beer lager, and order it by the pint or half pint, and discovered that most of Cool Britannia's capital city is closed by 11 at night, it was time to look for employment before any more of those hard-earned Aussie dollars slipped like water through my fingers. I'm a journalist, and had heard from friends that sub-editing work was available on national newspapers, so I made this my main line of attack.

There are many opportunities for work in Greater London. As a middle-class visitor from another affluent Western country, and therefore less likely to overstay your visa, you may not even have to prove you can work legally. Although I volunteered to some potential employers the fact that, due to the good fortune of having a British father, I didn't even need a visa and had the right to work, I was not asked by any employers if I was legal, nor asked to show any papers proving my status.

Some of the work, while reasonably easy to come by, is very badly paid. London is teeming with Australian nannies, pub workers, security guards, casual labourers and the like, all of whom earn a pittance. Some of these jobs come with live-in accommodation, which makes the low wages a little easier to bear.

As a sub-editor, however, I quickly picked up employment that was similar to newspaper work in Australia but paid much more. Even accounting for London's steep prices, I still had a higher disposable income than at home. Other skilled occupations I encountered among expats that seemed to be particularly marketable were accountants, school teachers, English as a second language teachers, hairdressers, nurses, doctors and other health workers and lawyers.

How did I go about it? I brought with me from Australia some written references, garnered from about four years of experience on Australian suburban and daily newspapers, and copies of my educational qualification, an arts degree. A journalist friend from my home town, Melbourne, who had preceded me to London by about a year gave me the names of various people on national newspapers who had given him work. I wrote job application letters to all of them, accompanied by copies of my references, and followed these up with phone calls. Within a couple of weeks I was working regular sub-editing shifts at *The Times*. One job led to another, and I ended up staying in London for four and a half years, working in both full-time and casual positions on several national newspapers.

I found work quickly for several reasons, some of which you may be able to use in your favour. I arrived in 1990, just before the end of the last economic boom when there was plenty of work around newspapers, and became known to a couple of employers who continued to hire me after the recession hit. Because London is such a big city, and also the media centre for the UK, there are many times the number of newspapers and magazines, and sub-editors' jobs, than there are in any Australian city. I arrived in June, just in time for summer, so newspapers were looking for fresh casual staff to fill in while regulars went on holiday. This factor also comes into play again at Christmas time. British newspapers traditionally use a high ratio of casual staff to permanents compared to their Australian counterparts. They try you out for a couple of shifts, and if you swim rather than sink, they ask you back.

This last factor is to your advantage when you're trying to get a foot in the door, but to your disadvantage if you decide to stay on indefinitely in Britain and make the leap from casual to permanent employment. Australian backpackers seem to pick up some sort of work easily, and have a reputation for being good workers. (This, I suspect, has more to do with the resourcefulness required when setting up shop in a foreign country than nationality. I've since heard similar comments about British backpackers being good workers in Sydney, where I now live.) However, even if you can make it into permanent employment you will probably find that the widely-held belief that all Australians are just passing through will hold you back from any promotions. This, of course, becomes a self-fulfilling prophecy: Australians who would like to stay in the UK leave because they find they have no career prospects.

Incidentally, although my friend's contact names were helpful as I looked for work, they were not crucial. If I hadn't had these names I would have sought the names of as many newspapers and magazines as possible from either a media guide at the local library or the White or Yellow Pages. As a reporter I'd already discovered that phone books are excellent research tools for all sorts of information, and that includes prospective jobs. However, you will probably have to access a copy at the post office. Phone books are as scarce as hens' teeth elsewhere; the reason for this remained a mystery to me.

Apart from collecting references and copies of my qualifications, I did no research on work prospects before I left Australia. As it turned out, I walked into work very quickly, but it would be better to be prepared. Before you leave Australia, find out the names of potential employers, the British professional associations for your occupation, and any contacts you can gather through word of mouth. If you can hit the ground running and find work quickly you'll be spending the pounds that you earn rather than those puny antipodean dollars. If there's not work around in your field you'll soon find that out, and may decide to keep what money you've got for more interesting past times than fruitlessly looking for a job.

For myself, I was astonished at my high rate of pay compared with what I had been earning in Australia. However, living costs are also truly astonishing—and not all salaries will be higher than at home. My very rough rule of thumb is that one pound buys you in London what one dollar would at home, and there are about two and a half dollars to every pound. Still, by living reasonably frugally in share houses I was able to travel to Europe several times a year and returned to Australia with more money in the bank than when I left.

This brings me to the thorny question of British banks. If possible, open a bank account before you go. Unless British banks have radically changed in the past few years, they are even less user-friendly than their Australian counterparts. Basic bank accounts all seem to have an overdraft built into them, giving the account holder access to, say, £50 of credit. This means that the requirements for opening an account are more stringent than they would be for an Australian-style savings account. As I started to collect pay cheques, which my employer's bank wouldn't cash, I needed to open a bank account, and fast. Some hope! First I needed a referee—someone who had lived in the country for at least a year and who was prepared to provide details of their banking to my bank—before I could even fill out the application form. It took three or four months before I could open the account, despite the fact that by then I had more than two thousand pounds' worth of pay cheques in my hot little hand (it took this long for my bank to check my referee's bona fides.) I pointed out this delay to my bank on a number of occasions in an attempt to speed up the process, but they just didn't seem very interested in my money. My pay cheques remained untouchable as I drew on savings from home. When the bank finally deigned to accept my money it took another three months before they trusted me with a card for money machines. Avoid this tiresome charade if you possibly can.

Another practical matter you have to grapple with is accommodation. Like so many before me I slept on a couch at a friend's place before I encountered the grotty world of budget London housing, which often made me feel I'd stepped into one of those aforementioned 1960s British black-and-white movies. I'd always thought that bedsits, for example, were self-contained studio flats, but they are actually single furnished rooms, maybe with a gas ring and a sink, and with a kitchen, bathroom and pay phone shared with the other tenants. They are as common today as they are in those old films in which the protagonists, played by the likes of Tom Courtenay or Alan Bates, make the trek from the north of England (actually a few hours by train) to try their luck in the capital, where they run into Julie Christie or Eleanor Bron on the stairs of their boarding houses. Other options are often unfriendly share houses, where everyone keeps to themselves and each has their own groceries in the kitchen, down to four separate bottles of milk in the fridge (the obsessive ones mark the milk level with biros), being a boarder in a flat with its owner, who may or may not make you feel at home, and squats, which are cheap but extremely basic. Share houses filled with a changing population of wall-to-wall backpackers (if it's Tuesday it's my turn to sleep on the sofa bed) are also popular with Australians. These have become quite notorious in London, and have even been the subject of TV documentaries.

I didn't live in an Aussie household, instead sharing with locals, and still remain in contact with one of them. Yes, there is such a thing as English reserve. Most of the friends I made were other Australians, and this was the experience of most people I knew. It takes quite a while to get to know work colleagues, and there is less out-of-hours socialising—BBQs, sporting teams and the like—than there is in Australia. An English friend, incidentally, the only English work colleague that I've stayed in touch with, told me once about taking her kids to the Christmas party for the children of staff. The children at her table, being children, chatted animatedly with all and sundry, while their parents did their level best to ignore each other as usual, a task made harder by their offsprings' friendliness. It's the same outside the office. The chat between strangers or nodding acquaintances that is part of our everyday life in Australia, and no doubt New Zealand—complaining about the weather with the newsagent, or exchanging pleasantries with the checkout operator—is largely absent in London. Striking up a conservation with a stranger is seen as a sign of madness.

Along with British reserve, bad food is another adjustment you will need to make. The 'New British' restaurants you might have read about in the food sections of the weekend supplements could cost your weekly pay packet. Otherwise, expect food to be worse than it is in Australia, whether it's a sandwich, a takeaway pizza or a sit down meal in a restaurant. After a while I gave up expecting good food when I ate out, and thought I was coming out ahead if the setting was pleasant and the service OK. Alternatively, brush up on your own cooking skills as the supermarkets have an excellent range of produce and groceries. Better still, eat curries since Indian restaurants are the best cheap-eats standby. Steer clear of the many workers' cafes, where overstewed tea and coffee served in old chipped cups and greasy chips come with everything else.

Now, let's say you decide to stay on in England for a number of years. You're a legal resident, you've found a good job and you've built up a circle of friends. You will then find that while you've been living away from home for so long, home has changed. Friends have got into a routine that no longer includes you, the prodigal traveller. As paths diverge people acquire different experiences and memories. In particular, friends back home are more likely to have married, settled down, had kids, and be living lives very different from yours as a footloose traveller. Loved ones among your parents' generation might not even be around any more.

Do keep in touch with friends and family back home and if you plan to stay away for a few years try to get back for visits, every year if you can manage it. Accept that your relationships with people back home aren't set in aspic. When you return maybe you'll pick up with friends where you left off; on the other hand, maybe you won't.

So the food's bad, the housing's mediocre and the natives are unfriendly and it's all a long, long way from home. Why work in London? For me there were two drawcards. The first was the city's rich history and culture, encountered everywhere. I remember rushing off to my first day's work in London, at *The Times* in the East End. The nearest Underground station was Tower Bridge, and I sped out of the exit, running late, only to be stopped short by the well-preserved remains of the city wall from Roman times, and beyond that, the Tower of London. Not all the history is ancient, of course. On another occasion I was on a bus travelling to a friend's place. As we went over a zebra crossing I noticed a crowd of tourists in front of a graffiti-covered wall and a building behind it with a sign saying EMI Studios, then a street sign, Abbey Road. Aaahh ... it was THAT zebra crossing. Serendipitous stumbling across such landmarks remained a delight all the time I lived in London.

The other drawcard was, as the real estate agents say, location, location and location. You can catch a cheap flight out of London to just about anywhere. I do miss flying to Amsterdam for the weekend. Or spending a few days in Rome. Or a fortnight in Egypt. An Australian friend of mine, who's become a long-term resident of London, regularly takes advantage of frequent and speedy ferry services to drive to France to visit friends, just for lunch.

In hindsight, a third benefit of a prolonged working holiday in London, or anywhere else for that matter, goes back to that sense of no longer being on the familiar autodrive of your life at home. You do have to start your life from scratch again, and if you don't have the twin strengths of resourcefulness and self-reliance you had better develop them pretty damn quick. Once you've got them, these qualities will stand you in good stead for life.

Volunteering in the UK

Susan Griffith

Any potential traveller to the UK is familiar with the images on countless calendars: country houses, luxuriant gardens, cobbled and thatched villages, castles and moats. But these icons of British history and landscape require constant upkeep, which relies to a great extent on volunteer labour. Visitors from overseas are welcome to join one of the myriad of projects which undertake tasks as diverse as repairing dry stone walls in the Lake District to guiding visitors around a National Trust property.

If the needs of people strike you as more worthwhile then a multitude of British charities can use willing volunteers to work with children and adults who have physical disabilities or social disadvantage. Opportunities abound, especially during the summer months, when organisations such as the Winged Fellowship Trust and Mencap's Holiday Service recruit volunteers to help at their holiday centres for people with special needs. If interested in this type of work, send two international reply coupons to the Royal Association for Disability and Rehabilitation (RADAR) requesting their information sheet 'Voluntary and Paid Opportunities for People Looking for Work With and For Disabled People and Disability Issues'. The Winged Fellowship Trust has centres in Southampton, Southport, Redhill, Nottingham and Chigwell, and pays for board, lodging and travel within the UK for foreign and British volunteers.

Free food and accommodation in exchange for some duties are a great bonus in London. Charities like Support and Housing Assistance for people with Disabilities (SHAD) and Independent Living Alternatives recruit full-time volunteers to assist people who have severe physical disabilities to live independently in the community. Volunteers are required to stay for a minimum of three or four months, and in exchange they receive a place to live and an allowance of at least £55 per week plus expenses. A shift system is worked by volunteers, allowing plenty of free time to explore London.

Many interesting projects invite volunteers to join them for just one or two weeks. Volunteering during a vacation may at first seem a contradictory idea—clearing debris from footpaths or singing songs with disabled children is not many people's idea of a holiday—yet participation in a voluntary project can be a very satisfying as well as an illuminating break from routine. Participating in a worthwhile project overseas benefits the foreign volunteer at least as much as the individuals or community being assisted, often in unexpected ways. Those whose primary motivation is to find an enlivening and challenging break outside the normal sphere of tourist operations are amply rewarded.

Some volunteers join projects for pragmatic reasons, to gain relevant experience in a field they intend to pursue such as social work or environmental management. For those concerned with career relevance, many kinds of voluntary work can feed into more permanent positions. A huge range of skills can be learned from a stint of voluntary work, from practical building skills to running a theatre project.

If you are keenly interested in a specific field, it is always possible to engineer a relevant job, provided you are willing to work without pay. Foreign travellers have been known to attach themselves to glamorous organisations like theatre companies, publishers, museums, website designers and the like simply by asking. A letter enquiring about unpaid work experience (what Americans call 'internships'), while agreeing to pay your own expenses but asking for help in finding accommodation in local homes, might well work and might eventually lead to paid work. Some who have succeeded are pleasantly surprised to find that Brits do not always conform to type; hosts are often friendly, trusting and helpful to those willing to help themselves. You can find these contacts in directories and telephone books.

Choosing a project

Community Service Volunteers (CSV) is probably the largest agency in Britain, placing 3000 volunteers in people-centred projects around the country. CSV caters for volunteers from overseas and places people of all nationalities aged 18 to 35 years alongside British volunteers in hostels and day centres working with people who need extra help with daily living. The placement fee for those applying from outside Europe is £499. Food, accommodation, pocket money (£24 per week) and travel expenses from the point of entry are paid for the duration of the attachment, usually between four and 12 months.

Many other organisations in the UK which require volunteers for varying periods are listed in the *International Directory of Voluntary Work* and in *Volunteer Work*. For summer-only opportunities consult the annual *Directory of Summer Jobs In Britain*.

After selecting the opportunities which attract you, it is simply a matter of contacting the organisation for details. Much can be discerned from the tone as well as the content of the literature produced by volunteer-seeking charities and organisations. For example, the glossy brochure of Earthwatch is an instant give away that joining one of their projects will cost a lot of money. This contrasts sharply with the printed-on-a-shoestring directories sent by the main UK workcamp coordinators like the International Volunteer Service (IVS).

Homestays and work-for-keep arrangements

Some travel clubs make it possible for travellers to stay with one another, providing an excellent platform for finding out about local volunteering possibilities without having to pay for accommodation. Every city and town of any size has a Volunteer Bureau or Volunteer Centre (contact details may be found in any Yellow Pages), which welcomes enquiries from temporary residents as well as permanent ones, though the majority of opportunities available locally will be part-time. Like all employers, the administrators of charities and organisations prefer face-to-face meetings to assess the contribution that a prospective volunteer is likely to be able to make.

Membership of the UK-based Globetrotters Club for £15 (£12.50 for students) brings with it a list of addresses of club members in the UK, many of whom are willing to host antipodeans. The organisation Servas International runs a worldwide program of hospitality exchanges for travellers, to further world peace and understanding. No money is exchanged between hosts and travellers and normally you don't stay with one host for more than a couple of days. To become a Servas traveller or host, Australians should contact Servas Australia, pay a fee of $65 and arrange to be interviewed by a coordinator.

Another hospitality club, Women Welcome Women World Wide, is aimed at women travellers and enables women from different countries to visit one another. There is no set subscription but the recommended minimum donation is $30 which covers the cost of the membership list and three newsletters in which members may publish announcements.

With growing fears about genetically modified foods, the organic farming movement is attracting an ever-expanding following around the world. Organic farms throughout the UK take on volunteers to help minimise or abolish the use of chemicals. The coordinating body goes under the name of WWOOF: Willing Workers on Organic Farms. WWOOF is an exchange; in return for your help on organic farms, gardens and homesteads, you receive meals, a place to sleep and a practical insight into organic growing. The active Australian branch of WWOOF can provide details or you can simply join the UK branch of WWOOF. Membership of WWOOF UK costs £10 per year and includes a subscription to their bi-monthly newsletter which contains small advertisements for opportunities both in Britain and abroad.

Communes (which are now more properly called communities) may provide a good opportunity for people sympathetic to a back-to-basics lifestyle. A directory called *Diggers and Dreamers* has details of communities in Britain as well as abroad and is available for £10.50 (£11.50 overseas) from Edge of Time, BCM Edge, London WCIN 3XX.

Buddhist communities throughout Britain run retreats either for a modest fee or on a work-for-keep arrangement. For example, the Losand Dragpa Centre in the Pennines requires volunteers to assist with various projects maintaining the Victorian castle in which it is housed. Also in Yorkshire is the Madhyamaka Centre where volunteers receive free dormitory accommodation, vegetarian meals and the chance to attend evening meditations and teachings in exchange for 35 hours of work per week.

Workcamps

Workcamps accept unskilled short-term labour and provide volunteers with the means to live cheaply while becoming involved in useful community work. For a contribution (£55 is average, £35 for students), volunteers can join a 10 or 14 day workcamp, which may range from an inner city gardening scheme to a project for people with special needs in rural Scotland. The main agencies coordinating workcamps are International Volunteer Service (IVS), Concordia, Youth Action for Peace, United Nations Association and Quaker Peace and Service.

A wealth of conservation projects attract volunteers for varying durations, from a weekend repairing dry stone walls to a longer attachment to a wildlife reserve carrying out animal counts, tree planting or pond clearing. No single project is going to save the golden eagle or a threatened wetland habitat, but it will allow the volunteer to stay in some of Britain's most remote and beautiful regions at little cost.

Several national bodies arrange working holidays or workcamps where volunteers of all backgrounds gather to carry out a specific task. Volunteers are usually housed in rough-and-ready base camps with about a dozen volunteers from all backgrounds, including a sprinkling of foreign volunteers, in each camp. Volunteers normally pay for their own transport to the site (though sometimes minibuses are laid on) and provide their own sleeping bags. A fee is charged to cover expenses, typically £50 per week. Evenings and one day each week are left free for socialising and exploring the local area.

The British Trust for Conservation Volunteers (BTCV) is the most important organisation working in conservation (and the counterpart of the Australian Trust for Conservation Volunteers in Ballarat). BTCV and its Scottish associate organise 600 working holidays to locations anywhere between the Anglesey coast of Wales and the Scottish Highlands, most lasting either a weekend or a week. There is more choice in summer, though projects run year round in England, and from March to November in Scotland.

The book *Green Volunteers* by Fabio Ausenda lists more projects and organisations through which both short-term and long-term volunteers can work with wildlife and habitats.

Protecting Britain's heritage

The National Trust for the Preservation of Places of Historic Interest or Natural Beauty in England (to give the National Trust its full name) was founded in 1895. Much of the Trust's work involves safeguarding the natural environment, and it relies heavily on volunteers who join working holidays lasting two, three or seven days to carry out this work. Projects take place year round. Most summer projects cost £53 to join whereas out-of-season working holidays cost £45. A few camps called 'Venture Holidays' last two weeks and are designed for international volunteers; the cost of £78 includes a program or visits and tours.

For volunteers interested in the routine maintenance and conservation of old buildings, contact Cathedral Camps. The Festiniog Railway Company in North Wales operates a famous narrow gauge railway. A new hostel accommodates volunteers in comfort. Many of the volunteers are steam engine fanatics, but anyone is welcome, however ignorant of signals and couplings, and will be put to work on non-railway related work like gardening or building maintenance. Other historic railways looking for volunteers are the Strathspey Railway Company in Aviemore and the Weishpool & Lianfair Railway, both in beautiful parts of the country.

Anyone who wants to participate on an archaeological dig should subscribe to *British Archaeology* for £19, available from the Council for British Archaeology. There are five supplements to the magazine called 'CBA Briefings' which list archaeological digs that may need volunteers.

Medical experiments

As with the expression 'working holiday' so 'paid volunteer' might be considered a contradiction in terms. Pharmaceutical companies, however, offer payment to volunteers who are willing to subject their bodies to unknown drugs. There are an estimated 55 clinical research units in the UK, according to the Association of Independent Clinical Research Contractors, many of which rely on testing their drugs on human guinea pigs. The demand for willing volunteers is so great that some of the larger pharmaceutical companies like SmithKline Beecham advertise in the mainstream media. Drug testing is overseen by ethical committees, but many people fear that the long-term consequences of taking unlicensed drugs cannot be safely predicted.

However, many people rely on drug testing to give their travel funds an occasional boost. You can earn as much as £100 per day and, if interested, it is worth checking noticeboards and making enquiries at any teaching hospital, or asking any medical student you happen to meet. To obtain details of SmithKline Beecham's program of experiments ring the Volunteer Recruitment Line on 0800 328 4195. Other contacts are found at the end of this chapter.

In most cases, volunteer subjects must produce a medical certificate from their own doctor attesting to their good health and foreign volunteers must prove that they are in the UK legally. If you are accepted and places are available on a particular study, you must undertake to abstain from all medications, nicotine, alcohol, tea, coffee, cola and chocolate for 48 hours prior to and following the test. Between swallowing the experimental medications and having tests (e.g. blood tests and blood pressure measurements) you will be given lunch and entertained with TV, videos, pool tables and the like.

Contacts

Community and social projects

RADAR, 12 City Forum, 250 City Road, London ECI V8AF.

Community Service Volunteers, 237 Pentonville Road, London NI 9NJ. Tel: (0171) 278 6601 or toll free in the UK: 0800 374991. Website: www.csv.org.uk.

Winged Fellowship Trust, Angel House, 20-32 Pentonville Road, London NI 9XD. Tel: (0171) 833 2594.

Mencap's Holiday Service, Optimum House, Clippers Quay, Salford Quays M5 2XP. Tel: (0161) 888 1200.

SHAD Haringey, Winkfield Resource Centre, 33 Winkfield Road, Haringey N22 5RP. Tel: (0181) 365 8528.

SHAD Wandsworth, 5 Bedford Hill, Balham SW12 9ET. Tel: (0181) 675 6095.

Independent Living Alternatives, Trafalgar House, Grenville Place, London NW7 3SA. Tel: (0181) 906 9265.

Conservation and heritage

British Trust for Conservation Volunteers, 36 St. Mary's St, Wallingford, Oxfordshire OXIO OEU. Tel: (01491) 839 766. The brochure line is (01491) 824 602. Website: www.btcv.org.uk.

Scottish Conservation Projects Trust, Balallan House, 24 Allan Park, Stirling FK8 2QG, Scotland. Tel: (01786) 479 697.

Earthwatch Europe, 57 Woodshock Road, Oxford OX2 6HJ. Tel: (01865) 311 600. Fax: (91865) 311 383. Website: www.earthwatch.org.

Royal Society for the Protection of Birds, The Lodge, Sandy, Bedfordshire SG19 2DL. Tel: (01767) 680 551.

National Trust, PO Box 39, Bromley, Kent BRI 3XL. Tel: (0181) 315 1111.

Cathedral Camps, 16 Glebe Avenue, Flitwick, Bedfordshire MK45 1HS.

Festiniog Railway Co, Harbour Station, Porthmadog, Gwynedd LL49 9NF, North Wales. Website: www.festrail.co.uk.

Strathspey Railway Co, Aviemore Railway Station, Dalfaber Road, Aviemore PH22 1PY. Tel: (01479) 810 725.

Welshpool & Llanfair Railway, The Station, Pool Road, Llanfair, Powys SY21 OSF. Tel: (01938) 810 441.

Council for British Archaeology, Bowes Morrell House, 111 Walmgate, York YOI 9WA. Tel: (01904) 671 417. Website: www.britarch.ac.uk.

Workcamp organisations

International Volunteers for Peace (IVP), 499 Elizabeth Street, Surry Hills NSW 2010. Tel: (02) 9699 1129. Fax: (02) 9699 9182. IVP has information on IVS workcamps in the UK. Directories of UK workcamps from the other coordinating bodies are available in April. These include:

Concordia Youth Service Volunteers Ltd, Heversham House, 20-22 Boundary Road, Hove, East Sussex BN3 4ET. Tel/fax: (01273) 422 218.

Quaker International Service Projects, Friends House, Euston Road, London NW1 2BJ. Tel: (0171) 663 1043. Fax: (0171) 663 1045.

United Nations Association, International Youth Service, Welsh Centre for International Affairs, Temple of Peace, Cathays Park, Cardiff CG1 3AP. Tel: (01222) 223 0888. Fax: (01222) 665 557.

Youth Action for Peace, Methold House, North St, Worthing, Sussex BN1 11DU. Tel: (01903) 528 619. Fax: (01903) 528 611.

Homestays and work-for-keep

Globetrotters Club, BCM/Roving, London WCIN 3XX. Email: info@globetrotters.co.uk.

Servas Australia, PO Box 1086, Airlie Beach Qld 4802.

Women Welcome Women World Wide, 88 Euston St, High

Wycombe, Buckinghamshire HP11 1LT. Tel/fax: (01494) 465 441. Website: www.womenwelcomewomen.org.uk.

WWOOF Australia, Mt Murrindal Cooperative, Buchan Vic 3805.

WWOOF UK, PO Box 2675, Lewes, Sussex BN7 1R. Website: www.phdcc.com/sites/wwoof/national.html.

Losang Dragpa Centre, Dobroyd Castle, Todmorden, West Yorkshire OL14 7JJ. Tel: (01706) 812 247.

Madhyamaka Centre, Kilnwick Percy Hall, Pocklington, Yorkshire YO4 2UF. Tel: (0159) 304 832.

Pharmaceutical clinics

Charterhouse Clinical Research Unit, Royal Masonic Hospital, Ravenscourt Park, London W6 OTN. Tel: (0181) 741 7170.

Glaxo Wellcome Pharmacology Unit, Level 7, Northwick Park Hospital. Tel: (0181) 864 3322.

Guys Hospital Drug Research Unit, 6 Newcomen St, London SEI. Tel: (0171) 403 3756. (Always looking for volunteers.)

Hammersmith Research, Central Middlesex Hospital, Acton. Tel: (0181) 963 4502.

International Clinical Trial, 99 New Cavendish St, London W1. Tel: (0171) 436 8080.

Royal Free Hospital, Pharmacology Dept, Hampstead. Tel: (01710) 830 2405.

Kent & Canterbury Hospital. Tel: (0800) 515 267.

Leicester Clinical Research. Tel: (0116) 273 3553.

Volunteering on Hadrian's Wall

Dianne Hoggins

'Going to have a little dig then, are you love?' enquired the middle-aged woman in the sensible coat and knitted beanie. She sat next to me clutching her shopping bag.

I tried to explain again that I was on my way to work as a volunteer on Hadrian's Wall. She smiled and nodded.

Through the bus window glimpses of the wall appeared against the classic British greenery. At times it was easily confused with the quaint dry stone walls of the farms. The original Hadrian's Wall, about three metres wide and five metres high, had run for nearly 130 kilometres across the north of England. The Roman Emperor Hadrian initiated its construction almost 2000 years ago to separate the Romans from the Barbarians.

Hadrian's Wall is one of the many archaeological sites in Britain which takes volunteer workers. Many organisations arrange work on digs of this kind or on other special projects. The Hadrian's Wall dig was arranged through the Youth Hostels Association, in conjunction with the National Trust.

'Once not twice brewed, driver,' yelled my neighbour. 'Hey love, here's your stop. Good luck!'

'Thanks, see you later,' I called as I got off the bus, realising what an inane expression this is for the many people who you meet in your travels but will never see again.

Volunteers on the Hadrian's Wall dig usually stay at the Once-Brewed Youth Hostel, close to the small town of Twice-Brewed, which is really one pub. In the huge hostel we sat around the fire chatting to volunteers from many different countries and to walkers who were following the route of the famous Pennine Way. Digging began early the next day, so we saved conversations for later.

'Oi! Go away!' Septimus, the dig's resident rabbit, hopped over to investigate the contents of my 'finds tray'. His nose twitched at the small shards of pottery, a plastic bead and some aluminium foil. The rabbit's namesake, Emperor Septimus Severa, was largely responsible for my presence at this particular site. He had ordered the rebuilding of great sections of the wall when, late in the second century and soon after its completion, the original wall began to disintegrate. The mortar his men used is still strong and British scientists are investigating its composition in the hope of copying it.

Few startling new finds were expected during our dig, as many extensive excavations have been made previously, particularly by Clayton in 1852 and Simpson in 1907 and 1933. The present investigations were mainly to examine the effects on the foundations of the vast number of tourists who walk along the wall each year; however, we were also exploring some small sections which had not been excavated previously.

New work required meticulous care with a trowel and brush, but other areas involved digging about two metres down to the wall's foundations with picks and shovels. As we got into the rhythm of trench digging, a New Zealand volunteer working next to me continually made references to the First World War and kept singing Vera Lynn tunes. This was not appreciated.

'What are you doing?' one was asked at least a million times a day by curious tourists, locally known as 'grockles'.

'Digging home to Australia,' one was tempted to retort, especially in the heat of the day. However, I wanted to share my fascination for ancient sites and made time to explain our purpose.

Most of the work was near Housesteads Fort, one of the most interesting and extensive sites along the wall. Its greatest claim to fame is its well-preserved latrines, complete with a flushing tank. The tasteless postcards depicting them in use by Roman soldiers are one of the biggest sellers at the local Heritage Shop run by snowy-haired women.

Important finds have been made at Hadrian's Wall. During a wet day we were shown some of the more precious ones: ancient brooches, a gold and carnelian ring, bone-handled knives and various pottery items. The prospect of unearthing finds like these maintains your energy levels far beyond the point where fatigue would normally make work impossible.

At the end of each day we trudged home across the rolling green fields and climbed stiles over dry stone walls. The archaeologist led the way, carrying her neurotic parrot which could not be left at home alone. Following her with picks and shovels propped on shoulders and buckets in hand we felt like the seven dwarves. 'Hi ho, hi ho, it's home from work we go.' Perhaps Yuppy, Sleazy and Randy, the modern day dwarves enjoying their working holiday.

When you complete your time on the dig, remember to get a letter of recognition to enable you to get work easily on other sites. That is, if you ever recover from aching archaeologist's back, rough archaeologist's hands and archaeologist's sunburn in the 'smile' between your shorts and T-shirt. I'd certainly try it again any time!

A Scottish Conservation Project (SCP) job was next on my agenda. I'd heard about this organisation in Australia but I was surprised to find few tourists take advantage of the variety of SCP programs. Both the SCP and the British Trust of Conservation Volunteers are super ways to get an in-depth experience of Britain, to meet people and to do something worthwhile for the environment. It's also cheap.

After a lunch of haggis and chips at Ullapool, a picturesque fishing and tourist town on the north-west Scottish coast, I hitched in a garbage truck to Inverpolly National Nature Reserve. Perched on a precipitous hill, overlooking the mountains of Stack Pollaidh, Cul Beag, Cul Mor and Loch Sionascaig, was the Knockan Cliff Trail, the goal of our project. The team's job was to replace the rotting wood of the duck-board walkway through the reserve.

My co-volunteers were mainly Brits on holiday: ten days' full board in the Scottish Highlands for $50. A comfortable, spacious cottage was our home during the project. It bordered onto a birch forest shrouded in moss and lichen; great for early morning walks.

A sustaining Scottish breakfast of porridge started our day followed by a picturesque drive to the worksite.

The boarding had to be carried up the cliff from the road, sawn into lengths and then nailed into place. Sounds easy, but there was much to learn. The new jargon words, stobs, stringers and decking, and the names of many tools I'd never even seen before, wrecking rods, stob straighteners and various saws, were easy to learn. Much harder to master was the art of efficiently sawing wet wood and driving nails in a vandal-proof (thumb-retaining) manner.

There were many different tasks and ultimately everyone found their own niche. At the end of the day we'd pile into Gertrude, the bright blue SCP Landrover, affectionately known as the 'vomit comet'. We'd drive the 24km through the Highlands, their peaks looming above us, to our 'home sweet home', cook a communal meal, or venture to a nearby beach for a BBQ or the local fishermen's pub to listen to tall tales.

During August the days were long, and vivid purple blankets of heather covered the moors and mountains. A big minus was the midges: clouds of tiny demonic blood-sucking gnats. They came in waves at various times of the day and sometimes work had to be postponed as we sheltered from their onslaught. Midges invade everywhere: ears, eyes, nose, one even found its way into my watch face. Some people recommend March to May as the best time to visit the highlands as the weather is pleasant and there are no midges. I'd rather put up with the midges and enjoy the spectacle of the purple heather-covered hills, but this thought is only in hindsight.

SCP projects allow at least one free day. We packed lunches and set out through the spongy peat, across streams and around peaceful tarns to the peak of imposing Suilven. I didn't make the summit but it didn't matter; just being in the vast expanse of the ancient Scottish Highlands and feeling I'd done my bit was enough.

Time off

Bryan Havenhand

Let's face it, you're not going to the UK just to work. The great thing about working in the UK is that the UK pound is a heavyweight currency compared to Australian and New Zealand dollars. A pound will take you further, and living on Europe's doorstep, you'll be able to go to Paris for lunch. That's not mythology, it happens!

Before launching into holiday possibilities, the issue of when you work and when you holiday needs to be addressed, in particular, when you holiday in the UK and when you holiday outside the UK. A change in working holiday rules a couple of years ago means that from the time you first enter the UK on a working holiday visa, the two year visa period starts ticking over. Before the rule change you could literally 'stop the clock' on the two year visa period when you left the county and start it ticking again when you re-entered the UK. Of course, if you are on a patriality or ancestral visa, or a British or European Union country passport, this limitation doesn't apply to you.

Things are getting tougher for working holiday makers as UK authorities become more forceful in policing the rules. In particular, this happens at entry points to the UK, especially Heathrow and Gatwick airports. For example, if you have been in the UK for nine to 12 months and go for a holiday to France you can expect some serious and detailed questioning from immigration officers upon your return. The immigration officers will assume, rightly or wrongly, that you have been working the whole time you have been in the UK and now intend to continue working, thereby possibly breaking the rules of the working holiday visa, i.e. you are only allowed to work for a total of one year during the two year period covered by the visa. The author knows of a case in which such questioning has been fairly intense and not very pleasant. In this case the person being questioned had abided by the rules of the working holiday visa. To avoid these situations, work for the first 12 months, holiday in the UK and then leave, or decide to holiday outside the UK during the early stages of your working holiday.

Passes

Before leaving home make sure you have all the passes mentioned in chapter two. Most of the visitation passes to museums, galleries and historic sites are available through the British Tourist Authority (BTA) in Sydney and Wellington. These will almost always be cheaper when purchased at home and even when they are not, you'll avoid long queues. Some queues like those weaving their way into Madam Tussaud's during summer are seriously long and require a lot of commitment; you might easily be standing there for an hour. Join the National Trust because Australian and New Zealand members are able to gain free or discount access to National Trust properties in the UK. The various travel passes are available through your travel agent and include air, rail and coach passes. Get the lengthiest Visitor Travelcard available. Join the YHA for access to over 320 hostels throughout the UK. Check with the BTA at the time you intend leaving to see what else may be available. The bottom line is to purchase as many passes as possible before leaving home. If you think this is an expensive exercise, wait until you get to the UK!

Information

You'd be a little crazy to head off to the UK without reading up on the possibilities offered by your travels. A little planning has never interfered with spontaneity but no planning can ensure you miss out on a lot. As mentioned elsewhere, go for a Lonely Planet or Rough Guide, they both have a nice ambience about them. Both have a number of editions covering London, the UK and Europe or a combination of these. There are probably more travel guides to London than any other city so you won't be short of sources, either very general or very specific, depending on your preferences. In London, you'll find bookshops in popular tourist areas, like around Covent Garden, which are full of guides to London and the UK on just about any theme you can think of, from architecture to walking. The Australasian press in London has plenty of information on what is happening but *Time Out* magazine (www.timeout.com) is the best weekly for a complete coverage of what's going on in London. In other cities you'll rely more on the local newspapers and the travellers' grapevine to keep up with things.

The *Independent Hostel Guide* is an annual guide published by The Backpackers Press in Bath. This guide lists 216 hostels throughout the UK that are not in the YHA International network. If you can't find it in bookshops in the UK you may need to order it. See the appendix for details. Also check out www.hostels.com.

The BTA in Sydney and Wellington provides information on the UK, and sells passes, basic tourist guides and maps, mostly published by tourists boards or the AA (Automobile Association). There are also plenty of websites: use a search engine or directory with key words relevant to your search. Alternatively, you could start with www.visitbritain.co.au.

The UK has some 800 Tourist Information Centres (TICs) scattered around the country. The main TIC in London is at 1 Regent Street, London SW1 and is open from 9am to 6.30pm during the week and from 10am to 4pm on weekends. It includes a complete booking service for air, coach and car travel, accommodation, theatre and sightseeing tours. There is an information desk for Scotland, Wales and Ireland along with a bookshop that also sells maps. You'll find local TCIs throughout the country wherever you see the *i* symbol. As in many countries, white lettering on a brown sign denotes a tourist drive or an attraction considered significant.

If you have specific interests, join a local group before leaving home to obtain some contacts in the UK or find a group in the UK that shares your interest and join up. Otherwise do something completely different, something you have never done at home. Take full advantage of living in Europe!

London

London alone can keep you occupied for a year without effort, although this really depends on how curious you are and how much stamina you have. There are all the traditional things to check out, the places and events that the world comes to visit, the monuments, the museums and galleries, the castles and the pageantry. On top of this is the continual passing parade of theatre, music, cultural activities, sporting events and celebrities. Not only do people go to London to see and experience things, they go to perform. From buskers to principals in opera companies. You can catch up with performances from home as antipodean rock bands, music ensembles and theatre troupes are frequent visitors to London. Go to a big soccer match or catch an antipodean rugby team, or the annual AFL dust up at the end of the Australian season. Get to Wimbledon on a half-price ticket. The options are endless.

The rest of the UK

When working in London it is easy to forget that a whole country exists outside of London. Australians, more so than New Zealanders, will be quite blasé about travel distances in the UK (and Europe), but don't underestimate the time taken to travel, especially by car. Once off the motorways, roads are often narrow and winding, and closer to London or major cities they will carry a lot of traffic. One of the author's most tiring driving sessions ever was driving back towards London on narrow roads at night with heavy oncoming traffic. Give me an Australian country road any day or night. The motorways are fast but new scenery passes pretty quickly. Another disincentive to travel by car is that the price of fuel is at least twice that in Australia.

There are now some 25 private operators of trains in the UK—the result of the breakup of British Rail—and while service hasn't improved dramatically, prices have increased. (The only train system in public ownership in the UK is the London Underground.) While train travel outside London is quite expensive, it is possible to significantly reduce the cost by travelling at odd hours or by booking and paying ahead. If you book and pay a fortnight ahead you can often get a fare that approximates a coach fare. However, with so many train operators the complexity of ticket types has increased considerably, so you'll need to learn the system to make the best use of it. Make sure you get your Britrail pass before leaving home; check out the options with your travel agent.

The cheapest way to travel throughout the UK is to make use of the National Express coach network which connects over 1200 towns and cities. There are a number of Explorer passes available and these can be purchased when in the UK. Telephone 0990 010 104 for more information when you are in the UK. If you are eligible, get a National Express Young Persons Discount Coachcard, available to those under 25. This card can be purchased in the UK and it gives a 30% discount on regular fares. Check the National Express website at www.nationalexpress.co.uk. Don't forget the independent travellers' bus lines such as Slowcoach which runs a hop-on and hop-off service around the most visited parts of the UK; telephone (01249) 891 959 when in the UK for more information. The ticket costs about £100 and has no time limits. Haggis runs a similar hop-on and hop-off service around Scotland; telephone (0131) 557 9393 when in the UK or check out www.haggis-backpackers.com.

Alternatively, purchase a bicycle! You can cycle around the UK with relative ease and you'll get fit in the process. The National Cycle Network aims to offer 8000 miles or close to 13,000 km of safe, signposted cycle routes by 2005 with almost 5000 km to be completed by June 2000. Contact Sustrans, PO Box 21, Bristol BS99 2HA or telephone (0117) 929 0888 for more information. You could even walk the length of the UK along designated walkways and finish up at John O'Groats on the northern tip of Scotland.

Europe

Continental Europe is barely a hop, skip and jump from London and two hours air time will see you in most parts of Western Europe. A few days or weeks away between work contracts is a great way to go, though you may prefer an extended period of travel. Some recruitment agencies offer loyalty programs which include discounts on various travel options if you stay with the agency long enough. London is full of travel agents including so called 'bucket shops' which offer dirt cheap air tickets but inevitability these tickets have no flexibility. So if you want to purchase tickets that are 'as cheap as chips' beware as the conditions attached to these tickets are pretty non-negotiable if you need to make changes later. You might look for charter flights operated by companies such as Britannia. These fly to the most popular destinations from the UK including Spain and the Greek islands.

The are plenty of tour operators running reasonably priced tours through Europe including Top Deck and Contiki. Top Deck is found at 131-135 Earls Court, London SW5. Tel: (0171) 370 4555 while Contiki is found at The Royal National Hotel, Bedford Way, London WC1. Tel: (0171) 637 0802. Website: http://contiki.com. These types of tours are ideal if you want some travelling companions or prefer someone else to look after the hassles of organising travel and accommodation. Alternatively, if you'd like to do it more independently, Busabout is an unlimited hop-on and hop-off coach that travels through many parts of Europe. Tel: (0171) 950 1661. Website: www.busabout.com. Don't forget the European train network but to get any value from this make sure you have a Eurail pass of some type. Talk to your travel agent about the options. You might even find it useful to have more than one Eurail pass if you intend to have a number of shorter excursions to the continent.

Lots of your travel options will evolve as you suss out the UK and your work options, meet people and make new friends. Make the most of it!

Working in Ireland, the Netherlands and Malta

Bryan Havenhand

These countries are included in this book because they are all in Europe and within easy reach of the UK, and they have working holiday visa options for antipodeans. Ireland has a working holiday visa for Australians and New Zealanders while the Netherlands and Malta have working holiday visas available to those on Australian passports only. Needless to say, you should organise your working holiday visa before you leave Australia, except in the case of the Netherlands where recent changes have allowed Australians to file a working holiday visa application with the Dutch Embassy in London. It is quite possible that after the completion of a working holiday in one country, you may choose to undertake another working holiday in one of the other European countries offering a working holiday visa.

Ireland

The Irish working holiday visa for Australians and New Zealanders has been available for a long time but has not been very popular simply because work in Ireland has been scarce. When unemployment in Ireland was around 14%, the working holiday visa application form warned applicants that finding work was not easy. A few years ago it was not unusual for the Embassy of Ireland in Australia to process only 50 visas per year. In New Zealand the annual allocation of visas was not usually filled. However, Ireland's economy has turned the corner and unemployment is now below

7% and those on working holiday visas are finding that short-term casual work is quite accessible. This is because Ireland has averaged an annual GDP growth rate over the past nine years of 6.8%, the highest in the world. As a result the embassy is currently processing about 1000 visas each year and in New Zealand there is strong competition to obtain one of the 250 visas allocated annually.

Applications for the Irish working holiday visa (which cost $60 or NZ$70) are considered if applicants meet the following key criteria:

- have Australian or New Zealand citizenship (i.e. you must hold an Australian or New Zealand passport)
- are between 18 and 25 years of age (up to 29 in some cases)
- are single or married but without dependent children
- have evidence of $1500 in funds plus a return air ticket or, in the case of the purchase of a one-way air ticket, $3000 in funds. For New Zealanders, this requirement for 1998/99 was NZ$2500 plus a return ticket or NZ$3500 with a one-way ticket.

The visa is valid for 12 months, but holders cannot work for any one employer for more than three months, hence the work is essentially casual or temporary in nature. Upon entry into Ireland you must be able to provide evidence to immigration officials that you have sufficient funds, at least for the initial period of your stay. There is a provision for those between the ages of 26 and 29 years to apply for the visa if they can provide evidence of a degree, diploma or trade certificate or otherwise show evidence as to why application was not made earlier. The embassy recommends that you obtain private medical insurance to cover hospitalisation costs in the event of an accident or illness.

If you or your parents (this applies to Australians and New Zealanders) were born in Ireland, you are eligible to apply for an Irish passport. If any of your grandparents were born in Ireland, you should contact the Irish Embassy or Consulate General to see if you are eligible for an Irish passport.

Contact: Embassy of Ireland, 20 Arkana Street, Yarralumla ACT 2600. Tel: (02) 6273 3022. Fax: (02) 6273 3741. Consulate General of Ireland, Level 2, Dingwell Building, 87 Queen Street, Auckland. Tel: (09) 302 2867. Fax: (09) 302 2420.

Type of work

As outlined in Margaret Toohey's article, 'Irish Times', hospitality work in hotels, hostels and restaurants is a prime area of employment for working holiday-makers. Work in childcare is an area available to women with qualifications or experience. Not surprisingly, given that much of Ireland's substantial economic growth in recent years is based on IT industries, there is a shortage of skilled IT staff. Jobs of this kind can be found in centres like the purpose-built International Finance Services Centre in Dublin. However, unlike the City of London, Dublin is pretty self sufficient in terms of accountants and financial staff. Given that IT work often fits well with short-term contracts it is a viable option for those with a working holiday visa.

The Netherlands

Like Ireland, the Netherlands has one of the most vigorous economies in Western Europe with an unemployment rate of less than 4%. Interestingly, about 30% of all workers are part-time, in part because married women are only now beginning to seriously enter the workforce. In addition, school runs from 8am to 1pm, meaning mothers are usually at home in the afternoon.

The Dutch working holiday visa for Australians has been available for many years but is not well known with maybe only 500 issued annually. Upon arrival in the Netherlands, work is not easy to find, the process of registering with authorities is tedious and bureaucratic (the process to legitimise any employment can take up to two months) and not many Australians speak Dutch. However, English speakers have little to complain about given the amount of English spoken in the Netherlands. You should have accommodation organised and enough money to cover your first two months in the Netherlands.

Applications for the Dutch working holiday visa are considered if applicants meet the following key criteria:

- have Australian citizenship (i.e. you must have an Australian passport)
- are not married
- are between 18 and 25 years of age
- have proof of a return air ticket or funds to purchase a return airfare
- possess and show proof of funds of at least $2000 to be used in case of inadequate earnings from employment.

This working holiday visa allows you to work for up to 12 months with the objective of combining a holiday with work experience. If you know people in the Netherlands who are prepared to assist you while you're there, this will help with your application. There is no charge for the visa. You should allow at least four weeks for the visa to be processed.

Upon arrival in the Netherlands you need to report to the local police station within eight days and apply for a temporary residence permit which costs NLG125. (At the time of writing $1 was equal to about NGL1.4.) You then collect your Dutch residence permit at another visit to the police station two to three weeks later. If you intend staying longer than three months you are required to register at the local town hall. This requires an original birth certificate authenticated by the Department of Foreign Affairs and Trade. This registration allows you to obtain a tax file number (a So-Fi number). Australia and the Netherlands have a healthcare agreement that allows Australians to receive free basic healthcare in the Netherlands after registration with the ANOZ Verzkeringen. Full details are available in the 'Thinking of travelling overseas' brochure available from Medicare offices or by ringing 132 011. This cover is not a substitute for travel insurance.

When employment is found, the employee is required to apply for a temporary employment certificate (NLG200) through the appropriate office. This certificate will bear the name of the employer and is not transferable to another employer. The employer must obtain a permit from the Ministry of Social Affairs. All suitable applicants who are EU nationals are considered before those who are non-EU nationals, so even labouring work at peak periods, such as at harvest time, may not be readily available.

Contact: Royal Netherlands Embassy, 120 Empire Circuit, Yarralumla ACT 2600. Tel: (02) 6273 3111. Fax: (02) 6273 3206. Email: nlgovcan@ozemail.com.au. The Sydney Netherlands Consulate General is located at 500 Oxford Street, Bondi Junction NSW 2022. Tel: (02) 9387 6644. Email: nlgovsyd@S054.aone.net.au.

Type of work

Unless you can line up a short-term contract in the IT area or find work in one of the many Dutch trading companies, most likely you'll find work in the hospitality or horticulture industries. Opportunities in hospitality are found year round in Amsterdam or during the summer in tourist destinations. In horticulture most work is available during harvest time but pay will be low. Some limited advice can be obtained from Stichting Uitwisseling en Studiereizen voor het Platteland (Foundation for Exchange and Educational Travel), Postbus 97, 1860 AB Bergen, The Netherlands. Tel: (072) 589 6144. Fax: (072) 589 4008.

Malta

The Maltese working holiday visa for Australians has been available since July 1995 but is not well known. With a population of about 380,000 on an island about 200 km^2 in area, opportunities are bound to be limited. English and Maltese are the two official languages and Maltese is the only Arabic idiom to use the Latin alphabet.

Applications for the Maltese working holiday visa (which cost $60) are considered if applicants meet the following key criteria:

- have Australian citizenship (i.e. you must have an Australian passport)

- are between 18 and 25 years of age (up to 30 in very special circumstances)
- are single, though married couples without children are eligible
- have a Police Clearance Certificate (apply at your local police station)
- have proof of funds of at least $4500 (this includes funds for a return airfare).

Visas are multiple entry and are valid for 12 months from the date of issue of the visa. In other words, apply just before you go but no less than six weeks before your intended departure. You can do any type of work provided your prospective employer obtains, on your behalf, an employment licence from the Department for Citizenship and Expatriate Affairs.

There is a reciprocal health agreement between Australia and Malta which provides for healthcare in Malta for up to six months from your date of arrival. Australians requiring medical attention should visit a health centre or see the general practitioner on duty at the Accident and Emergency Department at St Luke's Hospital. Full details are available in the 'Thinking of travelling overseas' brochure available from Medicare offices or by ringing 132 011. If you are staying longer than six months you will need to take out private medical insurance or have an appropriate level of travel insurance (which is advisable in any case). Remember that your travel insurance may not cover you while you are working.

Contact: Malta High Commission, 261 La Perouse Street, Red Hill ACT 2603 or PO Box 3510, Manuka ACT 2603. Tel: (02) 6295 1586/1645. Fax: (02) 6239 6084.

Type of work

The only type of work available (ignoring the lucky break) is in the hospitality industry during the summer (June through to September) when many tourists from Northern Europe descend on Malta's sunny shores. This includes work in restaurants, cafes, hotels and hostels. You may also be lucky enough to find some low paid agricultural work.

Irish times

Margaret Toohey

I held my breath with longing when I stepped off the ferry in Dublin one crimson frosty morning. My roots were in this country. Would I feel something special here? Or was I being romantic and ridiculous? I had always been fascinated with Ireland and was hoping not to be disappointed.

As an Australian in Europe, London is the easiest roosting point. One can slip comfortably into the expatriate community, and benefit from the relative abundance of employment and support networks. For myself, there was no question of remaining in London to work after I had sampled the sparkle-eyed Celtic hospitality, their euphonious beguiling accents, and the astonishing beauty of the countryside. London by comparison seemed huge, dark, crowded and impersonal. English skies were low and grey, whereas just over the Irish Sea the skies were filled with windblown light, and grainy scarlet sunrises. Not that it didn't rain, sometimes it seemed it would never stop, but there was undeniably something special about the place. I loved Ireland more than I dared to hope.

When I told people I wanted to work in Ireland, they would look at me disparagingly, cite high unemployment figures and tell me how the Irish are emigrating all over the world because they cannot find work. Of course this is all true, but luckily it didn't put me off. I soon learned that there are always jobs for those prepared to look, more so if one is prepared for hard work with little financial reward. Ireland was not a career move, but rather a way to understand more of this captivating country.

Australians are required to secure a working holiday visa before they can work legally in Ireland. The Embassy of Ireland in Canberra issues six-month permits for Australians aged between 18 and 25 years who are single or married without children, and able to prove they can support themselves for most of their visit. The primary purpose of the visit must be tourism. Another way of working legally is open to those who can prove they have at least one Irish parent or grandparent. Australians in this category are entitled to an Irish passport and may live and work as an Irish citizen. Remember, Ireland is in the European Union, so anyone holding a passport of a member country can also work in Ireland.

The sort of work available in Ireland is often in the catering or hospitality industry. If you can wait tables and pull pints, or bluff and say you can—it doesn't take long to learn—then you are assured of work. Employers like to hire Irish workers, but my experience is that they will give you a go and hire you on your own merit. Dublin, for example, is full of restaurants, and an even greater number of pubs. All that is needed is a couple of afternoons of doorknocking and you will be onto some possibilities at least. The money you earn will keep you in Guinness with a roof over your head. Most importantly for a working holiday, it will put you in contact with Irish people, both as customers and workmates. I quickly discovered the radically different perspective employment gave me during my time in Ireland. I immediately shed my 'tourist' status, and started to look at life from the inside. I was earning local wages, joining a difficult local economy, reading local newspapers and becoming involved in local issues and opinions. If you are truly interested in experiencing what it is like to live in the Irish culture, then I think working in Ireland is essential.

In Dublin you might try asking for work at Bewley's Cafes (an Irish institution, and the erstwhile haunt of characters like James Joyce), or Abrekedabra fast food, as these have a high staff turnover and are quite willing to hire travellers. With regard to working in pubs, women may find they are relegated to 'lounge girl' status, clearing glasses and taking orders, as behind the bar is still often regarded as a man's realm, but this is changing. In the area of women's rights, Ireland is very much a society in transition.

Another option for work is childcare. Au pairs, nannies and mothers' helps are required, both live in and live out, and are relatively well paid, especially as this kind of work is mostly cash in hand. Agencies such as Poppins Nannies, Europlacements and Irish Nanny Services, all located in Dublin, report placing many

Australian and New Zealand women in the past few years. It is helpful to have a qualification in childcare, and also to hold a full drivers licence. Far more important is having references to prove previous experience, and committing to a time span, often as long as a year. All food and accommodation are provided, so your wage (about IR£70-110 per week) looks quite attractive.

Some people, particularly those prone to occasional bouts of homesickness, find security in being part of a family, though childcare work can be hard and the hours long. There is an obvious need for flexibility with a position such as this, but a common arrangement is to work five days a week and have the weekends and evenings free. In Ireland a nanny is treated as one of the family, on an equal social footing, unlike in other countries where you could be regarded as a servant or slave.

A lot of travellers in Ireland pick up work in hostels. This is poorly paid, and is more often work in return for accommodation. Hostels usually require people for cleaning and making beds, reception duty, and advertising. The latter job means hanging around the bus station with leaflets, pouncing on unsuspecting backpackers and luring them to your hostel before the opposition can get a look in. I found hostel work loads of fun—for a while at least. I met people from all over the world, and everyone was on holiday so the atmosphere was one of constant celebration. It is the only job I have done where I did not have to dress up and attempt to look like a respectable citizen. Hostel work can also be the key to living in remote and beautiful rural areas, and experiencing life as part of a small village community.

If you are interested in getting out of the cities, the *Blue Book of Irish Country Houses and Restaurants* (available free from the Irish Tourist Board, O'Connell Street, Dublin) is a good resource. It lists 30 or so guesthouses and restaurants, many located in areas of spectacular natural beauty. Generally open from Easter to October, these establishments are worth contacting for work. Local staff are employed each year, but often extras are required, and owners are not averse to hiring those from down-under. Most jobs in remote areas provide accommodation so are great if you are attempting to save pennies. However, all social activity centres on the local pub so working in a pub can be counterproductive to saving! The local is a magical place when you live in the community. Within its dark, smoky environs occur almost all of the gossip and storytelling, all of the fun and 'craic', and all of the music and dancing. There is a delightfully broad demographic of patronage, from infants to grandparents.

Yet another option for the fit and healthy who are interested in rural life is Willing Workers On Organic Farms, better know as WWOOF. (To join the Irish branch contact Annie Sampson, c/- Tulla PO, Tulla, County Clare, Ireland.) WWOOF supplies a list of addresses and brief descriptions of farms providing food and accommodation in return for assistance with farm work. Most of the farms are either entirely organic, or working towards this goal. Many cater for vegetarians and accept children on prior arrangement. All WWOOF does is put you in touch with the farmers, it is then up to you to make arrangements. WWOOFing is a great way to meet people, experience a different lifestyle (unless you have always lived on an organic farm!) and even learn new skills and crafts such as yoghurt, cheese or butter making and basket weaving. Most farms prefer a minimum commitment of one week, but you are under no contract and are free to leave at any stage. People report varying experiences, depending very much on the farm and volunteer's preferences. If rising every day at 4am to milk goats is not your idea of a good time, then don't apply to a goat farm! You don't need any qualifications to WWOOF, just a willing and enthusiastic disposition, a strong pair of wellies, and rain gear. WWOOFing can be arranged at very short notice, if necessary, and can extend for whatever duration is agreed to by you and your host farmer.

If you choose to work in Ireland you are in for a fabulous time. I found the Irish people have an amazing generosity of spirit and an unending capacity for enjoyment of life, with their tongues ever poised to tell a story, their throats full of song and a musical instrument never out of reach. For me the country was both welcoming and accessible, and I met other foreigners who shared the same experience. There is a feeling of liberation—even hitch-hiking was comparatively safe, though as with anywhere there are still risks.

I spent time on a remote island, where the hostel sat on the sand and the ocean seemed to lap in the bedroom at night. I danced in a green field overlooking a blue bay for three days, while the likes of Bob Dylan and Van Morrison played on an open stage. I pulled pints of Guinness and set them down on a damp wooden bar. I found in some ways a more innocent society: strangers at the bus stop always ready to converse, and outside of the cities not a car (or tractor) passed without a nod or a wave to the stranger on the road.

I realised one of the most important aspects of living in another culture is that it provides you with a basis upon which to challenge your own society. It can also provide motivation for change. I was in Ireland a long while, I had plenty of time to ponder and explore and realise that, in the words of Michael Leunig, 'Nothing can be loved at speed'. I loved Ireland all the more each day I spent there, for the things I learned about myself, and for the beautiful countryside. I learned too about the First World country which is the third poorest in the European Union (in front of Portugal and Greece). I saw the other side of emigration, the one we don't see in Australia because we only gain in diversity and talent from the incoming people. Ireland loses her finest, youngest, brightest and most talented because she cannot provide them with work.

Keeping busy in Amsterdam

Kerry Martin

Living overseas for any period of time is always an enriching experience, even if you don't realise it until long after you are home. You may find yourself overseas after being transferred for your work or it could be that one day you just decide you would like to try living in another country. Whatever circumstances lead to your overseas domicile it is bound to be worth it.

For me, it was a combination of the need for professional experience and just deciding to pack up and go. Working for a university in Australia meant that I was eligible for extended leave as part of my professional practice. Many private companies also provide the same opportunities for their staff. After a quick spin of the globe, I opted for Amsterdam as my first choice mainly because I had an offer of work there in a friend's company. I believe there are also good employment leads on the Internet especially via online newspapers like *The Guardian* and *Observer* which publish their complete recruitment sections on their websites.

I also chose Amsterdam because of its central location in Europe. Up until now, the distance and the cost had always kept my European holidays to a minimum. So, I intended to make the most of my new base with its handy location on the tip of Western Europe. Working in Europe would provide me with local currency which would make travelling a realistic option. Unfortunately for Australians and New Zealanders antipodean dollars won't buy much in Europe at the moment.

Having negotiated 12 months leave with the university I commenced preparations to leave Australia which, as I discovered, require a certain amount of effort. First, I had to organise a tenant for my apartment and convince friends that extra furniture could enrich their lives for a year. Then came informing the Tax Office that they would be poorer for the next 12 months. Of course, the banks and other usual suspects in control of my monetary affairs also had to be informed otherwise I feared that one day an ATM would eat my Visa card. Luckily Australia has a reciprocal medical agreement with the Netherlands so I did not need to take out expensive private health cover, although generally in the Netherlands medical care is of good quality and very reasonably priced. I ordered a new copy of my birth certificate, which is necessary when applying for things like tax file numbers and working permits in Europe, brushed the dust off my passport and headed for Tullamarine Airport.

Once in the Netherlands you have to obtain a So-Fi number to work. Once I had this I was set. Salaries in most of Western Europe are generally higher than in Australia but the downside is that you pay very high taxes, which is not so good for the short-term resident who won't reap the benefits in the long run. However converting your earnings back into Australian dollars upon returning home seems to make up for this.

I made a fairly soft landing into the Amsterdam way of life. The city is very accessible for the foreigner and I quickly found myself driving on the 'wrong' side of the car on the 'wrong' side of the road, just like a local. I was relieved to find most of the locals speak perfect English so you can be lazy and not bother to learn Dutch, although the road signs proved to be a challenge. If you decide to persevere, the University of Amsterdam has excellent short language programs. Even though the language is not a problem in most face-to-face dealings, national TV and radio are all in Dutch. The BBC and CNN are available but neither feature much news from down-under so at great expense I subscribed to Melbourne's *Age* which arrived fairly spasmodically, sometimes two on the same day, at my home in inner Amsterdam. For more instant news I would log onto the ABC News Homepage which gives excellent coverage of the important news. But after a few weeks I didn't bother, I figured if anything major happened it would be on the BBC. I knew I could live without Brian Henderson, but I knew I would not be able to survive a year without films, and I was relieved that the Dutch, unlike the rest of Europe, don't dub their films. One weekend I was in Germany and had a good old belly-laugh watching 'Melrose Place' in German. I actually think Amanda really could be German.

I worked for an international shipping company in Amsterdam but for a former journo, I had little preparation. However, I think most journalists could survive just about anything and the Dutch way of doing business is not all that different to home. Thanks to the universal language of Microsoft, I adapted quickly to Windows in Dutch, but found it best to concentrate on the icons rather than the words. (Still a kid at heart.) After years behind a screen, I could remember where to click the menu box if I wanted to save a file. I just had to stop myself from reading what was written in the familiar boxes as I had no idea what would happen if I were to 'Afdrukken' my file or 'Opslaan' it. Most of the time this worked and I only lost all the company files once, or was it twice.

After I had settled into work, I decided it was time to immerse myself in the Dutch way of life. A Dutch friend recommended an excellent book by Simon Scharma, *The Embarrassment of Riches*, which quickly gave me an insight into the Dutch psyche. As an Australian, I found the Dutch generally to be very frank and forthright, something we Australians cannot claim as a strong point. They are also a very hardworking bunch who not only work hard but play hard. There is not a Dutch equivalent of a sickie, it just doesn't sit well with the Calvinist hard working way of life. Amsterdam is a very relaxed city and there is an obvious and refreshing absence of suits and ties, so I was glad I had left my Armani at home. But don't be fooled by the casualness of the place —it is still a very serious centre of business and commerce even though wearing your Levis to work does take the sting out of the early morning alarm.

While the climate inside the office may be warm and relaxed nothing prepared me for the Dutch weather. Not even four years in Melbourne. It was lucky I arrived in summer so I had a month of warm sunshine before the cold hit. I even aired the cossie and shorts a couple of times. The warm weather quickly came to an abrupt end one Sunday early in July. I was told summer was now over, which meant the end of blue skies and sunshine. What! It was only July! I had to replenish my wardrobe with scarves, hats, gloves, thermal underwear and double-soled boots. I couldn't believe that winter had not officially started. The locals smugly told me it was their worst summer in decades but I didn't believe them. It does however seem true that Dutch TV weather forecasters lie so as not to depress the viewers too much. So a typical long-range weather forecast between July and February would be along the lines of 'some rain is expected in the late afternoon' when actually they knew it was going to piss down every day for eight months!

As a Victorian by birth I knew how to handle an umbrella, although I quickly learned that an umbrella is no protection against a Dutch hailstorm. Perhaps a metal rubbish bin lid would be better. In fact, there is no place for vanity in a Dutch hailstorm. Anything waterproof and rock proof is what's needed. For the locals this usually translates as a cardboard box if you're lucky enough to have one nearby. Naturally, you spend a lot of time indoors, which for an outdoor type takes some getting used to. The weather doesn't seem to bother the locals in the slightest, who still ride their bicycles on the bleakest of days. Of course they are wearing cardboard boxes on their heads.

As the bicycle is the way most of Amsterdam's residents get around, I didn't waste time getting back on a bike. I figured it was sometimes safer to be on a bicycle because I could avoid stepping in dog shit, of which there is an ample covering on the streets of Amsterdam. Although you would think from the spread of it that there were more dogs than people, there aren't. Actually the city has a larger cat population. They even have cat houseboats and a cat museum housed in a salubrious mansion on Amsterdam's Champs Elysse, the Herengraacht. While on the subject of museums, Amsterdam has a varied collection. Of course there is the world famous Rijksmuseum, which houses the world's biggest collection of gloomy Dutch masters, but there is also the Sex Museum and the Torture Museum for those who enjoy the lower end of the cultural spectrum. It was not surprising that it didn't take long for me to tire of the tourist areas. Away from tourist traps like the Leidseplein and the Rembrandtplein, a plethora of local bars and cafes abound in the narrow lanes and along the canals.

This brings me to the subject of Dutch food about which I will be brief yet kind. It sucks! Stodge with stodge. Try a pea soup with French fries, very healthy, or a Hutspot, a conglomerate of onions, carrots and potatoes—and nothing else! Hardly high cuisine. Thankfully the Dutch adopted some of the cuisine of their former colonies: Indonesian and Surinami foods are abundant although somewhat lacking in the good old chilli. Before I finish my whinge about Dutch food, it is also impossible to get a decent coffee in Amsterdam. There, that is it. But on the positive side the Dutch do have excellent cheeses, great mayonnaise and of course white beer, an excellent beer heavy with yeast and the taste of hops. Hardly a replacement for a good coffee in the morning though.

Generally the Dutch like socialising and I quickly found myself at home in the local 'brown cafes' where the air is thick with smoke, sometimes of the hemp variety, and the white beers are flowing. You may even be lucky enough to find a miniature billiard table. There is a lack of space in the city as most buildings within the old city are no more than three metres wide, which doesn't leave a lot of room to sink a ball. In any case, when I became accustomed to popping over to London or down to Paris for a weekend, I didn't have a whole lot of time for billiards. It was such a novelty being only 30 minutes from London by plane.

Being in Europe made me very aware of how isolated most of us are from our forebears. The time difference between Amsterdam and home seemed to mark out this distance.

After nine months I had well and truly settled into the Dutch way of life. With only three months to go before my return to Australia I had absorbed more experiences than I would have over several years in the cosiness of my Aussie comfort zone. So it must have been good for me. The exposure to a different way of doing things is the best lesson we can have. I have also learnt never to complain about Melbourne weather again!

Appendix

Metric - imperial conversion

Some more commonly used measurements:

Length

1 centimetre = .394 of an inch;	1 inch = 2.54 centimetres
1 metre = 3.28 feet;	1 foot = 30.5 centimetres
1 metre = 1.09 yards;	1 yard = .914 of a metre
1 kilometre = .621 of a mile;	1 mile = 1.61 of a kilometre

Mass

1 gram = .0353 of an ounce (oz)	1 ounce = 28.3 grams
1 kilo = 2.2 pounds (lbs)	1 pound = 454 grams
1 tonne = .984 of a ton	1 ton = 1.02 tonne

Volume of fluids

1 litre = 1.76 pints	1 pint = .568 of a litre
1 cubic metre = 220 gallons	1 gallon = 4.55 litres

Speed

1 km per hour = .621 of a mile per hour

1 mile per hour = 1.61 km per hour

Temperature

Degrees in Fahrenheit = (9/5 x °C) + 32

Degrees in Centigrade = 5/9 x (°F - 32)

Books

Working and living

Summer Jobs Britain (annual), ed David Woodworth, Vacation Work (www.vacationwork.co.uk). The Australian distributor of Vacation Work titles is Bookwise, 54 Crittenden Road, Findon, SA 5023.

Live Work and Play in London and the UK 2nd ed, Sharyn McCullum, 1996, Kangaroo Press.

The International Directory of Volunteer Work, ed Victoria Pybus, 1997, Vacation Work.

Working in Tourism: The UK, Europe and Beyond, Verité Reily Collins, 1995, Vacation Work.

London Guide (annual), *TNT Magazine*. Free publication available in the UK or in the BTA kit.

Living and Working in Britain 2nd , David Hampshire, 1996, Survival Books. Aimed at those wishing to move to the UK for the longer term.

Teaching Overseas for Australians and New Zealanders 2nd ed, Bryan Havenhand, 1997, Global Exchange.

Travelling

London, Pat Yale, 1998, Lonely Planet

London, Rob Humphreys, 1997, Rough Guides

Virago Woman's Travel Guide: London, Josie Barnard, 1994, Virago Press.

Great Britain & Ireland, a travel planner from *TNT Magazine*. A free publication available in the UK.

Scotland for Backpackers, Erica Brook, Reed Publishing (Edinburgh). Available in the UK.

Independent Hostel Guide (annual), Backpackers Press, 2 Rockview Cottages, Temple Walk, Matlock Bath Derbyshire DE4 3PG. £3.95. Available in the UK.

Cheap Sleeps Europe (annual), Katie Wood, Trafalgar Square. This lists 1000s of accommodation places of all types in 26 countries for less than US$20 per night.

Europe by Train (annual), Katie Wood, Trafalgar Square. Provides lots of details for the train traveller including rail pass options, some interesting tourist attractions in each major city or region and where to find tourist information.

Other

London, ed Jack Ian, Granta. Granta is a book/magazine with each issue focusing on a particular topic. Granta 65, focusing on London, is 352 pages long and includes fiction, reportage, memoir and photography of one of the world's great cities. $19.95. It is distributed in Australia by Allen and Unwin.

Rhyming Cockney Slang, Jack Jones, Abson Books. If you're struggling with the rhymes that make no sense (Hampstead Heaths is of course, teeth) then maybe this little book will help. £3.95. Available in the UK.

Index